GETTING STARTED IN
COMPUTER
GRAPHICS

GETTING STARTED IN
COMPUTER
GRAPHICS

GARY OLSEN

NORTH LIGHT BOOKS

CINCINNATI, OHIO

About the Author

Gary Olsen is the publisher of *Tracks*, published for the employees at Deere & Company's Dubuque and Davenport, Iowa, facilities. He is also the editor of *Dubuque Works Weekly* and the *Waterloo Weekly News*. In addition, Gary is an exhibiting artist, photographer and communications skills teacher. Gary has written and illustrated articles for the *Joe Williams' Report* and has written articles for *Pre-*, the journal of electronic prepress (South Wind Publishing).

Gary's publications have won honors, including the Gold Quill of Excellence from the International Association of Business Communicators.

Recognized for his illustration and design talent using computers, Gary has been commissioned to do work for such diverse companies as Sharp Electronics, Walt Disney Studios, Aldus Corporation, NEC, Tektronix Corporation and Wacom Technologies.

Getting Started in Computer Graphics. Copyright © 1989, 1993 by Gary Olsen. Printed and bound in Hong Kong. All rights reserved. No part of this book may be reproduced in any form or by any electronic or mechanical means including information storage and retrieval systems without permission in writing from the publisher, except by a reviewer, who may quote brief passages in a review. Published by North Light Books, an imprint of F&W Publications, Inc., 1507 Dana Avenue, Cincinnati, Ohio 45207. 1-800-289-0963. Revised edition.

97 96 95 94 93   5 4 3 2 1

Library of Congress Cataloging in Publication Data

Olsen, Gary
    Getting started in computer graphics / by Gary Olsen.
        p.   cm.
    Includes index.
    ISBN 0-89134-468-3
    1. Computer graphics.   I. Title.
    T385.O37 1993
    006.6—dc20   92-31063
                                                      CIP

Edited by Poppy Evans and Mary Cropper
Designed by Clare Finney
Cover Illustration by Max Seabaugh. "Raychem Man" © 1988 Raychem Corporation.

The permissions on page 148 constitute an extension of this copyright page.

To the person who is always supportive, keeps me organized and on task—my wife, Linda

A C K N O W L E D G M E N T S

The many artists who work with microcomputers and contributed to this volume are given credit for their work in a separate section. Their consultation, like their talent, was extremely valuable. However, I would like to focus attention on some special friends and colleagues who provided technical and artistic assistance in writing this book.

Kathleen Friel: My first editor and one of my closest colleagues in this endeavor. Her vision was integral in the organization of this material.

Mary Cropper (North Light): My editor on the revised edition. She made this book better. Mary worked very hard on this, and I am grateful.

Poppy Evans: An artist and writer, she helped me with the enormous task of revising and upgrading this material for the second edition.

Rich Theobald (MicroComputer Consultants, Dubuque, Iowa): Perhaps the most talented and knowledgeable computer hardware specialist in the country. He continually teaches me about the technology I am dealing with and he insists I've taught him a lot about graphics and design. Art meets science in the ideal symbiotic relationship.

Dr. Ed O'Neill: A surgeon and microcomputer expert whom I've been working with to combine computers and medical specialties. He's a dear friend and valuable resource of information on a wide variety of microcomputer platforms.

Linda Claussen: A fine artist who embraced the computer as an artistic medium during my book project and volunteered to test the painting and drawing lessons. She provided valuable help in cataloguing the many submissions contributed by artists.

Mike Saenz: From my first phone call to this gifted computer artist, I knew I was talking to a fellow maniac with a mission. His understanding of the power and significance of computer art is at a level clearly beyond most artists' current thinking. He is more than a computer artist. He's a futurist.

Aldus Corporation (developers and publishers of Page-Maker and FreeHand): It's such a class company. They are clearly the best software company as far as an artist and author looking for information and help is concerned.

Nancy Freeman, Lawrence Gartel and Louis Markoya: Talented artists working with the Amiga computer. They shared much of their expertise in using their favorite medium.

Laura Lamar and Max Seabaugh: San Francisco graphic artists who provided me with valuable contacts with other computer artists.

Jeff Goertzen: One of the most exciting illustrators working in newspapers today. Most readers of the *Orange County Register* (Orange County, California) probably have no idea that the spectacular and often fanciful drawings of this exceptional artist are executed on a computer.

Ron Chan: An artist for the *San Francisco Chronicle* whose work is reminiscent of the classic poster art of the 1920s and 1930s.

Chris Iburg (Tektronix, Inc.): Chris helped me with the color output of my artwork. Tektronix is another class company that happens to be in the computer printer business.

Tomoya Ikeda: An incredibly talented artist from Japan. I never thought I would meet this inspiration in person and then, at a MacWorld Exposition in San Francisco, I was introduced to him by Jim Woolum of Qualitas Trading Company. I was in awe. It was at that time, upon hearing of my project, that Tomoya agreed to participate.

Leona Breitbach: Special thanks for ironing all my shirts during this book project!

CONTENTS

Prologue

Introduction:
How to Use This Book
The most effective way to tackle this book—
for both novices and more experienced computer artists.
x

1
The Metaphorical Desktop
Understanding desktop drawing and painting tools, and
figuring out how they'll affect your work.
4

2
Tools of the Trade
How to select an affordable microcomputer, software
and printer for the kind of design and graphics
production you plan to do.
12

Demos:
Developing a Logo—Wildcat Run 36
Designing a Newsletter Banner—The Desert Quail 40

3
Painting and Drawing
The difference between preparing object-oriented graphics,
drafting graphics, PostScript drawings
and bit-mapped paint graphics.
42

Demo:
Combining Paint and Draw Programs—Dali 54

4
Drawing on a Microcomputer
Creating art with high-resolution drawing programs.
60

Demo:
Drawing in PostScript—The Rose 74

5
Painting on a Computer
Creating art with computer paint programs.
80

Demos:
Using Color Paint Programs—The Carousel Horse 92
Painting Textures—The Elephant 98

6
How to Work With Service Bureaus
Where to go when you want slides, high-resolution
page layouts, color separations, color proofs and solid
advice about making your work the best it can be.
108

Demo:
Creating an Illustration From a Scanned Image—
A Medical Illustration 122

7
Editing and Manipulating Photographic Images
Creating art with image-editing/manipulating programs.
126

Demo:
Image Editing—Mustang 144

Permissions 148

Index 149

PROLOGUE

And a mouse is a miracle enough to stagger sextillions of infidels...

Walt Whitman from "Song of Myself"

Since I began researching and preparing material for the first edition of this book in 1989, there have been changes in the computer graphics field. For one thing, personal computers have become more powerful. But remarkably, little has changed in terms of the basic tools or the "user interface" that most software makers adopted early in their development of rendering software. In other words, the onscreen icon for a pencil is still a pencil, a brush is still a brush, etc. Some of these tools may have become more powerful and versatile with the latest versions of the software, but they still look and act basically the same. That means all the rendering demonstrations I prepared originally for this book still work with the newest versions of software.

And nothing has appreciably changed in how best to approach a graphic project using the computer. Continue to approach the computer like any other traditional medium. You wouldn't start a watercolor or an oil painting without preparing a simple sketch or thumbnail, and you shouldn't start work on the computer without one either. Whether you prepare a PostScript drawing, a painting or even a three-dimensional graphic, the best strategy is to start with a simple bitmap cartoon of your composition. It can be a line-art drawing prepared in a basic monochrome paint program or a rough drawn with ordinary pen and paper that's scanned for importation into your favorite rendering program.

How has my life as an artist continued to change since I wrote the first edition of this book? In many extraordinary ways. For one thing, I no longer feel like a voice in the wilderness trying to legitimize the computer as an artistic medium. Instead, it has become a jungle out here! I have many new clients who seek my computer expertise. Where before I was pushing my clients to accept this new medium, now they are pushing me to be even more creative. The competition and the ever-improving quality such competition brings continues to astonish me. If I have any advantage at all over others pursuing this field, it is that I had a slight head start. I also continue to work with software and hardware companies, evaluating new products.

The computer has allowed me to branch out into new areas. One of the more interesting assignments I've had since the first edition of this book was published was the preparation of computer graphics for one of Disney's film studios. I had forty-eight hours to complete six concept drawings in full color. A fax, three phone calls and an overnight delivery later, I beat the deadline. It was a challenge, but true to the life of a computer artist, I never had to leave the comfort of my home studio.

Another area in which my computer has allowed me to branch out has been in textile design and silk-screen work. I discovered long ago that my computer's software gave me the kind of control over the color separating process that is key in preparing silk-screens. Finite control over line, fill, color blending, traps and chokes allows me to design complex graphics in stunning detail and quality. Now my work is seen on ready-to-wear garments sold coast-to-coast, all with designs prepared entirely on the computer. I don't think I would ever have become involved in such an enterprise without my computer.

The future for the graphic designer who embraces the computer is rich with opportunity. But I am still amazed at how ill-prepared some aspiring artists are to accept this new technology. Not long ago, I was asked to speak to a graduating class of artists and designers at a local college. I had spent days preparing my talk, and the essence of my message was "learn everything you can about computers." I was to be the third speaker and was so immersed in my own preparations that I don't recall who the first speaker was. But I'll never forget the man who preceded me—a vice president in charge of production for a major publishing firm.

He took the lectern and said matter of factly, "We see artists' work every day. We are in the midst of hiring artists right now, and I would be delighted to arrange interviews with you. However, I have one important question: 'Do you know how to use a Macintosh?' If not,

we really don't have more to talk about until you do."

The vice president couldn't have had a more devastating effect on his audience. (He blew my speech out of the water.) It was clear that most of the students had spent the last four vital years of their lives having fun with paints and pastels, but hadn't touched a computer for drawing and painting purposes. I'm certainly not saying they wasted their time. The best computer artists are those with solid grounding in traditional art forms. But how would you like to know you just spent four years or more on a degree and then discover that you may have to pursue more training to qualify for a job?

You, on the other hand, purchased this book. Can we assume that you are ready to pursue the extra personal training to become computer capable? Are you prepared to take a most important step in a journey that will make your creativity soar? Whether you are an artist desiring to explore the possibilities of the computer or a computer person desiring to capitalize on your machine's graphic capabilities, this book is for you. It will serve as a bridge between art and technology.

—Gary Olsen

INTRODUCTION

How to Use This Book

   This book's primary objective is to help graphic designers and artists develop their drawing and painting skills on the microcomputer. The computer, like no other artistic medium, has the power to wed creativity and technology.

   Artists and graphic designers are attracted to it for a variety of reasons, most dealing with productivity.

   Computer people, on the other hand, are attracted to picture mak-

ing because of the increased popularity of the so-called graphic interface. This term describes the screen graphics found on your computer that make the machine easier to use.

   This book is not going to duplicate the information already included in your software's instruction manuals. As an artist, I can attest that most software manuals are not much fun to read. This is probably because many manuals are written by technical people who assume

you already know how to draw. And you do, but executing art and illustration on a computer is like starting at ground zero.

   In the arena of computer graphic software packages, the instruction manuals are generally handy, and you should at least take the shrink wrap off of them. You'll be surprised how, in most cases, you can solve your problem quickly.

   Trying to supply current information about specific brands of software is difficult, because most com-

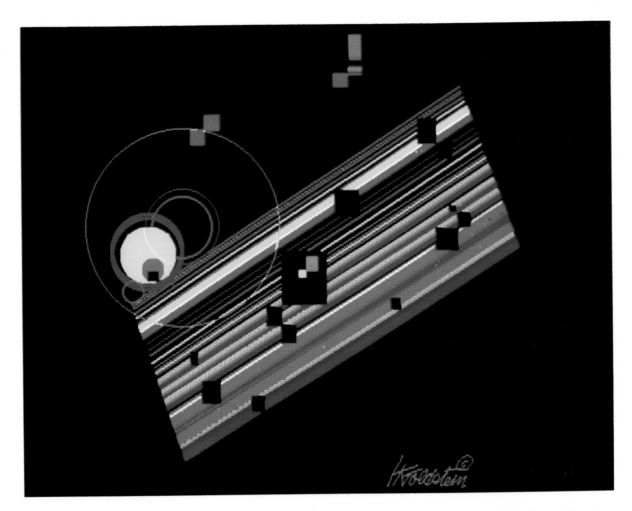

puter programs are modified, improved, and have features added as often as twice a year!

Fortunately, most graphic software programs, regardless of the brand-name computer used (referred to as the computer platform), operate with very similar onscreen tools. Most can be enhanced with an accessory like a stylus/tablet, and most use almost identical onscreen icons for graphic manipulation and transformation.

We've designed this book, therefore, to be used with virtually any drawing and painting software you choose. Your approach to this book should be first to familiarize yourself with your favorite drawing and painting programs, and then to tackle some of the lessons prepared for you on these pages.

This book is also designed for computer graphics novices—those who have considered purchasing a Macintosh, IBM or Amiga, and are curious to see the graphics potential of such a system. Your objective should be to improve your rendering skills directly on the computer.

Most art or graphics instruction books don't tell you how to hold your brush or how to swizzle it in your paint. They show you paintings being prepared from blank canvas or illustration board to finished composition. And that has been our strategy. When a drawing lesson tells you to "copy a line, flip it horizontally, and paste it somewhere on the screen," you should be able to do that without having this book show you where to put your fingers on buttons or keyboard.

Howard Goldstein, "Ode to Kandinsky"
(Above) Created using the Designer's Toolkit on a customized Apple IIe.

Don Woo, "Taj"
(Left) Created using Studio 8 on a Macintosh.

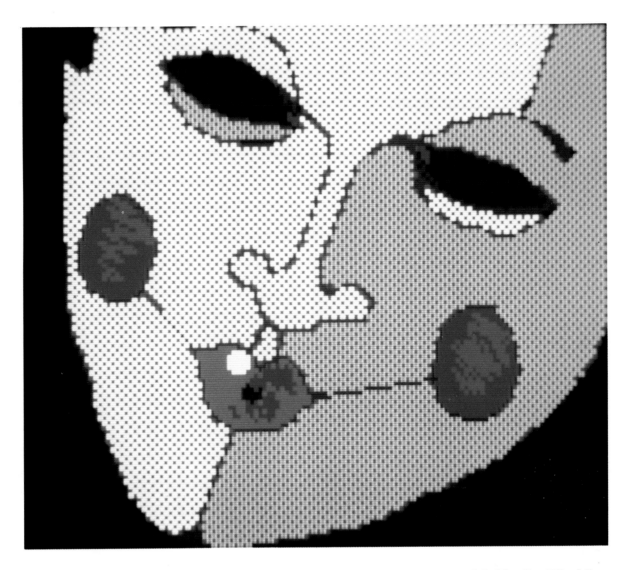

New in This Book

In this edition we've made a few changes to reflect the updated features of some of the software programs that have come about since this book was first written. We'll also discuss some programs and tools, such as Fractal Design Painter, pressure-sensitive tablets, and image editing/photo manipulation software that didn't exist then.

The Gear We Used to Publish This Book

This book was written, designed and laid out with Macintosh computers. My publisher and designer have Macintosh IIs and did the page layouts and pre-press work in QuarkXPress and Adobe Photoshop.

Here's the rundown on my computer hardware and software:
- Macintosh IIfx with 8MB of RAM and 210MB internal hard disk
- RasterOps 24-bit Graphics Card with 19-inch Trinitron monitor
- Wacom pressure-sensitive tablet
- Abaton Scan 300/Color scanner
- Tektronix Phaser II color printer
- Apple Personal LaserWriter NT
- SyQuest 44MB removable hard disk system
- Aldus Freehand
- Aldus PageMaker
- Aldus SuperPaint
- Adobe Illustrator
- Fractal Design Painter
- Adobe Photoshop
- Microsoft Word

Howard Goldstein, "Mask"
(Above) Created using the Designer's Toolkit on a customized Apple IIe.

Rachel Gellman, "Flight"
(Left) Gellman, a New York artist, created this wool rug design.

S S BREITBACH

G OLSEN

THE METAPHORICAL DESKTOP

. . . .

**Understanding desktop drawing and painting tools,
and figuring out how they'll affect your work.**

Until recently my experience as an artist has involved the more traditional tools of the trade: the pencil, pen, brush and pastel. Now, as I sit before my electronic canvas, I find myself working with metaphorical versions of the same tools.

The lessons I learned long ago about draftsmanship, composition, color harmony, value, texture, and the importance of light are still the most valuable assets I bring to this new medium. Yes, it's true. If you are a "natural artist" and already possess some drawing and painting talent, you have greater potential to create better computer pictures at a faster pace. Imagine yourself as an athlete bringing your natural ability to run, jump or catch a ball to a new sport.

Keep in mind that computer-prepared graphics represent an incredible variety of styles. Some computer artists work tirelessly to achieve gracefully smooth lines and fluid shapes, trying desperately to mask any hint that the work was

. . . .

Gary Olsen, "A Luxury Voyage"
This poster is a PostScript drawing and it demonstrates the use of color blending and graduated fills.

accomplished on a computer. But artists consciously try to capitalize on the computer's bit-map look, preferring to effect the Etch-a-Sketch quality of jagged lines and big pixels.

Most microcomputers have the ability to deliver a variety of resolutions. You must decide on your objective: Do you want smooth, seamless graphics, or will you accept the "digital aesthetic"?

INCORPORATING THE COMPUTER IN YOUR GRAPHIC DESIGN PROJECTS

If you are a designer or artist taking up the computer for the first time, it probably isn't wise to discard your trusty drawing table, templates, pencils, pens or hobby knife immediately. You may be faced with a problem that can be solved only with traditional tools. There is absolutely nothing wrong with going back to the drawing table.

However, my personal experience in learning to use the microcomputer has been what I describe as "complete immersion." I recognized immediately that this was an incredibly powerful and productive tool, and I chose not to gradually introduce the microcomputer into my design schedule or production routine. On a gamble, I completely shed myself of the old methods that involved pen-

cil comps, tracing vellums, PMTs and paste-ups. I made a commitment to make my computer investment work for me, come hell or high water.

Neither hell nor high water came, of course, and now I'm writing a book about the process—using desktop publishing tools, naturally. It was an often rough and bumpy ride and I ended up taking a lot of wrong turns, but the trip was well worth it.

START SMALL

A good introductory strategy in applying the computer to a design project is to start small. If you are going to use your computer for page layout, make your first project a brochure rather than a magazine. The smaller, more manageable project will provide nearly every kind of challenge you are to face, and you will likely attain a sense of accomplishment faster. You must be careful not to overwhelm yourself by biting off more than you can effectively chew.

If you are going to use the machine to prepare illustrations, try to resist the temptation to reproduce *The Last Supper* with all twelve apostles in complete detail and full color.

A simple logo or trademark job is an ideal starting point. It should

Louis Markoya, "Girl's Face (Helen)"
Markoya occasionally combines scanned images of family members to create interesting compositions on his Amiga. Amiga's ability to display 4,096 colors simultaneously makes it ideal for experimentation.

contain a simple graphic element and perhaps some type.

SCANNERS

A great concept, but sooner or later, you must learn to draw and paint on the computer.

At some time, most computer graphic artists will use a reference tool. A scanner is a fast way to bring a photographic or conventionally drawn image to your screen for modification, tracing, coloring or combining with other graphic elements.

Complicating the use of scanned images in your artwork is the potential for copyright infringement. If you are involved in commercial illustration or design, you need to acknowledge or obtain permission from the originating source of your reference material unless you created or commissioned the drawing or photo yourself. This could apply to

anything from a registered trademark to a celebrity's face.

The most popular application of scanned or video images in computer art is the transportation of a traditionally prepared sketch or drawing from paper to screen. Many artists still work out their ideas on paper first, and a scanner is an ideal way to import the graphic for combination with other graphic elements such as type. The scanned drawing can be cleaned up and colorized in some applications.

STILL VIDEO

Imagine a camera that contains a computer disk. You shoot the camera at your subject just like any still camera. The information can then be read by your computer, and the image electronically cropped, sized and pasted into your document. Consider this photography system without film or processing; with us.

Still video performs image capture with—what appears to be—an ordinary 35mm camera. The disk that records the analog image data is removed when it is full and inserted into a player that comes with the camera (or it could be part of the camera). The player "plays" the image, allowing you to edit it onscreen or print it out to a special printer that's also part of the complete system. Using a video capture or "frame-grabber" board in your computer, you can digitize the image from the player, which then allows you to format the photo for inclusion in your computer graphics or desktop publishing application. The implications of this technology in the graphic arts field are enormous.

Computers have been able to handle image capture from videotape for a long time, but still video is a different twist on the technology. First, the still video camera is much smaller than even the most compact video camera. The still video camera, like a 35mm system camera, can be equipped with lenses of any focal length, telephoto, wide angle, fisheye, etc. The system typically includes three components: a camera, a player and a printer. You supply the computer and the video frame grabber. The player can be attached to your computer for direct image transfer.

With powerful gray-scale and full-color photo retouching programs like Adobe Photoshop, Aldus Photostyler or Digital Darkroom, complete photo retouching is available on your desktop. This tool is extremely valuable for gathering and manipulating photo references for illustrations.

DRAWING, PAINTING AND IMAGE EDITING PROGRAMS
On a collision course.
From the very beginning, painting programs have been on a collision course with drawing programs.

P • O • E

G • OLSEN

"With such care and skill, a picture is at length painted which leaves in the mind of him who contemplates it with a kindred art, a sense of the fullest satisfaction."

Now several applications use the best of both. With the technical advancements in high-resolution color graphics displays and output devices, you can create illustrations with the resolution of a fine color photograph. Add to this environment useful tools such as a programmable color palette and the ability to create dramatic perspective and three dimensions at the click of a button, and the artist now

Gary Olsen, untitled
From a graphic arts viewpoint, the computer is an ideal medium for integrating type with your illustration. My wife is an English teacher and Poe is one of her favorite authors. I spied a photograph of him in one of her textbooks and asked her for a quote that had to do with art. This is the result of our collaboration.

**Nancy Freeman,
"Sad Gold Mirror Masks"**

(Above) Freeman created this image
using an Amiga computer. Her painterly
approach creates truly fine art that
extends the computer medium somewhere
beyond graphic design.

**Nancy Freeman,
"Ritual Figure"**

(Right) A painter who is totally at home
with a computer, Freeman doesn't try to
make computer art look like traditional
art. She works with large pixels as if they
were colorful mosaic tiles. This painting
was done on a PC with a paint program.

possesses drawing and painting power and productivity of incredible proportions!

Image editing software programs have the capability of retouching and manipulating scanned images. But if you think these programs are strictly for photo manipulation, you may limit yourself. Many artists use image editing software as their primary painting programs. The tools are identical to those found in painting programs, and image editing programs offer some painting features that aren't available in more traditional paint programs. For example, most of them offer a magic wand tool that lets you select a specific image area plus similar pixels in areas adjoining those you touched, transforming them all at once. Many artists feel the brush, airbrush and finger-blend tools in photo manipulation programs to be more versatile and precise than those in painting programs.

CREATING BETTER GRAPHICS WITH THE COMPUTER

Some computer artists have come from the ranks of the computer field. Others have migrated from the graphic arts. Drawing talent is drawing talent in my estimation, and it can come to the surface in all kinds of people.

Today's top computer artists and "screen designers" are really no different than the easel painter. The first step is to learn how to use

Don Woo, "Dragon"
This California artist used Studio 8 on a Macintosh to create this illustration.

Michael Gilmore, "Egyptian Games"
This packaging motif was created using FreeHand on a Macintosh.

the technical tools of the trade, whether it be the finest vine charcoal from Venice, Italy or an Apple Macintosh computer from Cupertino, California. And the measure of artistic success is based on how an artist arranges compositional elements. It doesn't matter whether you draw on a computer screen or a piece of paper. Good composition is what brings dynamic power to a piece of art. It draws the viewer into the piece and leads his eye to something specific the artist wants him to see.

In the graphic arts and commercial illustration field, the computer can be a tremendous productivity tool. When a piece of art requires modification, change of color, line thickness, scale, compositional elements or text elements, computer-prepared art can be changed with no extraordinary expenditure of sweat. But even more important are the pre-press options, image special effects, or animation tools that are available in several microcomputer applications.

Consider pre-press. You have the ability to output your image in perfectly registered color separation format directly to film for a color key and platemaking. Fewer photomechanical steps are involved compared to traditional pre-press.

THE FUTURE OF COMPUTER ART

Spectacularly beautiful and engaging images will be created that may never leave the screen! Today, most computer-produced artwork is destined to be published in ink on *paper*, mass produced in a manufacturing process, and then distributed. This communication process is slowly being eclipsed by a paperless world of information exchange. As television eclipsed radio, newspapers, books and periodicals as the masses' primary source for information and enter-

tainment, so will the computer find its place among the media in our society. It will happen, I suspect, as computers become more like appliances in the home.

One futurist predicts the computer won't even resemble today's box on the desk. The computer screen will be a pair of glasses with three-dimensional imagery. There will be no need for a keyboard, because you will speak your input. You will navigate through a three-dimensional world of information, networked with other people wearing similar devices, and you will manipulate graphic elements in that environment with electronic gloves, the ultimate relative pointing devices.

Computers will play an ever-increasing role in helping us control our complex environments. We've already learned how to depend on

them for certain types of information. The quality of microcomputer graphic displays is constantly improving, and powerful programs will be able to simulate graphically almost any vision a creative mind could conjure. Similarly, computer-synthesized music has come to dominate the recording industry.

The successful designer of the future will possess the knowledge to navigate effectively through this communications network. The skills of drawing and painting on a computer have already become just as legitimate as watercolor painting on a sheet of Arches paper. Yet in the future, most of these fantastic images will never grace a printed page, never leave the electronic consciousness of society's ultimate computer network.

Annette Weintraub, "Enfurl"
Weintraub, a professor at City College of New York, created this piece using Studio 8 on a Macintosh and then output it to a QMS ColorScript printer.

TOOLS OF THE TRADE

. . . .

How to select an affordable microcomputer, software and printer for the kind of design and graphics production you plan to do.

The question I'm asked most frequently by computer novices is, "What brand of computer is best for me to buy?" I must confess, I can't recommend any particular computer to you — at least not right off the bat.

Narrowing one's choices when it comes to a computer purchase can be difficult. If you're an aspiring computer graphic artist, most home or hobbyist computers won't be adequate. If you want to do computer graphics that ultimately will be output to a laser printer or similar high-resolution machine, you must choose a computer powerful enough to run programs that are intended to output to those devices.

Color is another consideration when selecting a computer. Color requires a computer with plenty of power (in the form of memory) to run the display and color palette. The better color paint and drawing programs require more than one megabyte of RAM (Random Access Memory) to run effi-

. . . .
Don Woo, "First Passage"
This is poster art for a Mac II paint program, SuperPaint by Aldus/Silicon Beach. Naturally the graphic was prepared using SuperPaint.

ciently. Also, you must understand what a good color graphics card can do in terms of the number of displayable colors you can simultaneously work with onscreen. And you must choose a storage device big enough to contain your software and the large, memory-hungry color graphics files that you no doubt will want to save.

WHICH COMPUTER?

My first truly graphic computer was a Macintosh I bought back in 1985. Though many of the programs I use on the Mac have counterparts on other platforms (it's not necessary to have a Mac to realize the benefits of this book), I found that my complete investment in the Macintosh platform over the years has generated an excellent return.

However, the rise of Microsoft Windows for the PC environment has made the choice of a platform with a user-friendly graphic interface less cut and dried. Recently I performed at a computer trade show for a client whose software runs on both the IBM and Mac platforms. I performed all of my demonstrations on the IBM, and I must confess that my client's software ran just as well as the Mac version. The software, which

ran on a Microsoft Windows operating system, had the same look and feel as that which ran on the Mac.

What does this tell you? That you should evaluate all platforms within your reach. Where computers once were distinguished by their features or abilities to perform tasks that others couldn't, the differences are fading fast.

Let's say you're making a decision about adopting a specific computer platform for your home studio to pursue a freelance computer graphics profession. Do you look at price? Features? Power? User-friendliness? Product support? Available software? All of these should be considered, but maybe you should consider these important criteria first:

1. Which computers do most of my clients utilize? Is your computer capable of easily formatting your graphics in ways compatible with the majority of your clients' computers?

2. Which computer platform and type of computer files is my service bureau most familiar with? Some service bureaus cannot handle native Amiga files, so you may have to make those files usable through an image-editing program such as Adobe Photoshop.

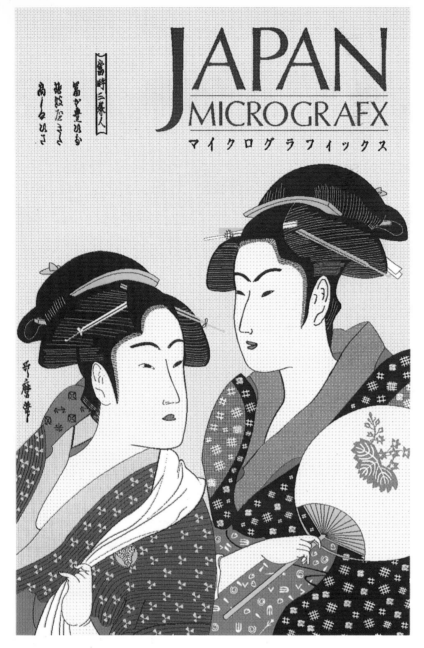

JAPAN
MICROGRAFX
マイクログラフィックス

David Haber, "Japan Poster"
Haber is a staff artist and designer for Micrografx of Richardson, Texas, the company that developed Micrografx Designer, a popular PostScript drawing program for the IBM PC. This illustration was printed on a Hewlett Packard PaintJet printer.

More brands of scanners or monitors available for your system provide a broad range of prices and competitive features.

Your specific needs as an artist are the most important factors to consider in picking a system. Those needs will determine how much processing speed, resolution and capacity you will use. Then it boils down to exactly what you can afford or are willing to spend. To determine what you'll need, ask yourself these three questions.

1. Can you specifically prioritize which tasks you wish to accomplish on a computer? (Example: publishing my newsletter, producing graphics for my newsletter, word processing for my newsletter, production management of my publishing operation, data management, and so on.) Don't be too general in terms of intended tasks. Envision yourself actually sitting down at a computer doing something you may currently do without a computer. Be specific!

2. Have you determined which software is the best to meet the demands of your number one task? Visit computer dealerships and software stores and try the products. Ask to have them demonstrated by a knowledgeable salesperson. And good luck, because truly knowledgeable computer salespeople are often difficult to find. It's not the computer stores' fault. How could any salesperson be knowledgeable about the hundreds of software applications the store sells? Just remember this: never, never, *never* buy an expensive software product without thoroughly trying it out first. And try out all comparable and competing software products on their respective computers.

There's no adequate computer dealer or software retailer in your area? Contact the software companies directly and ask if they can

3. Which high-end output device gateways are available for the system I'm choosing? If the publication is being assembled on a Scitex, Crosfield or Hell system, will my files navigate safely and smoothly through the assembly process?

4. Which systems are most of my local colleagues using? Is there a users' group I can belong to and obtain help from when I need it?

5. Which printers, scanners or other peripherals are available for the computer platform I choose? Which and how many third-party hardware companies support this platform?

send you demonstration copies of their product. Many have nonprinting demo copies of their software available (especially the more expensive programs). Now all you have to do is find a computer on which to run them.

The software reviews published in computer-specific magazines are an excellent resource, too. Most are very honest, pointing out a software program's foibles as well as features.

3. If you have figured out the best software for your main task, which computer runs that software the best? That's right, let software selection drive your hardware selection. Avoid letting hardware dictate the type of software you will buy. Compromise will often lead to disappointment. This is particularly important advice if you are selecting a computer to do graphics. You would be amazed at how many people purchase a computer based on the assumption it is the best because of a brand name or television commercial, only to discover (when it was too late) that it was inadequate for their needs or too difficult to operate.

Now That You've Zeroed in on a Computer, Customize It to Do Your Tasks Properly

Buying a computer is like going to an expensive foreign restaurant where you don't understand the menu and all the selections are a la carte. Particularly in the graphics arena, there may not be a simple turnkey, out-of-the-box system that can meet your needs.

Computers have become modular, much like televisions and stereo equipment. Instead of speakers, a tuner and a CD player, you now buy items such as Random Access Memory, a hard disk, a high-resolution monitor, an enhanced graphics card, or a CD-ROM drive.

James Dowlen, "Pacific Dreams"
Dowlen created this using Time Arts Lumena software on an Everex computer.

Max Seabaugh, "Plains Indian"
Seabaugh created this using SuperPaint on a Macintosh.

A MICROCOMPUTER'S COMPONENTS

A graphic microcomputer configuration is made up of the following main components:
• **CPU**—Central processing unit.
• **Screen, display or monitor**
• **Graphics card or frame buffer**— Drives the display screen.
• **Mass storage unit**—Floppy disk drive, hard disk, removable hard disk, a read-and-write optical disk drive.
• **Printer**—Impact printer, laser printer, ink-jet printer, pen plotter, image processor.
• **Scanner**—Scans photos, drawings, even three-dimensional objects, allowing you to import the image into a paint, draw or page layout program.
• **CD-ROM drive**—Plays specialized compact disks containing graphics, sound, even software.

• **Specialized mouse or computer drawing device**—Nonmechanical or optical mouse, joystick, electronic drawing tablet, trackball.
• **Auxiliary or backup drive**—Additional floppy disk, hard disk, cassette drive.
• **Telephone modem or network connection**—Enables you to exchange files and data with other computers nearby over a local area network or far away by means of the telephone.

An auxiliary media drive can be an extra storage device, a backup device that routinely carries complete copies of your precious files and software. It can also perform as a network server, sharing files among several computers connected by a network. Such devices can be a valuable backup for your computer data if a main component, like your hard disk, fails. Backing up your computer data files is necessary and can most often be accomplished using floppy disks.

Computer graphics are typically larger than text files in terms of memory required to display, modify and store them. Copying large files to floppy disks can be difficult since one complex graphic can exceed the capacity of a floppy disk. Consider using a removable harddisk device, which can record large amounts of data on portable hard-disk media in a removable cassette. It's ideal for large, memory-intensive computer graphics.

MISTAKES COMPUTER SHOPPERS MAKE

The following are the two most common mistakes made in buying computers for graphics applications:

Not buying enough memory. You may discover your high-powered color drawing software requires at least 2 megabytes of RAM to run properly, and you bought only 1 megabyte of RAM. For example, I currently run 8MB of RAM. Test

Bonnie Meltzer, "Wildflowers"
Hand-painted computer output from a
Macintosh.

your intended software first and check the RAM requirements in the program's documentation. Also, high-powered draw and paint programs get bogged down (slow screen refresh) as your artwork becomes more detailed. You need to look at a fast CPU and possibly an additional co-processor or accelerator board, which speed the computations that create your image on the screen.

Next, you need plenty of storage memory in the form of either an external or internal hard disk to store your programs and work-in-progress. It seems to be a fact of life: Someone invents better, more powerful, more feature-laden software, but it needs just a little more power to run efficiently. So the computer company increases the power, and you upgrade or buy a new computer.

My current machine is a Macintosh IIfx, whose CPU is based on the Motorola 68030 chip. Some of my art grinds the computer down to where I am impatiently waiting for screen refresh. To solve this problem, I must increase the speed of my computer platform.

I could buy a faster graphics display card to speed up screen redraw. But the CPU is what really makes rendering programs more productive. I could get a faster CPU by upgrading the motherboard or by adding a co-processor board. Each strategy has a good price/performance ratio. But do I want to make this kind of investment in a computer that I might want to replace with a faster one? As I write this, I'm looking at Apple's line of 68040 machines (the Quadras) that

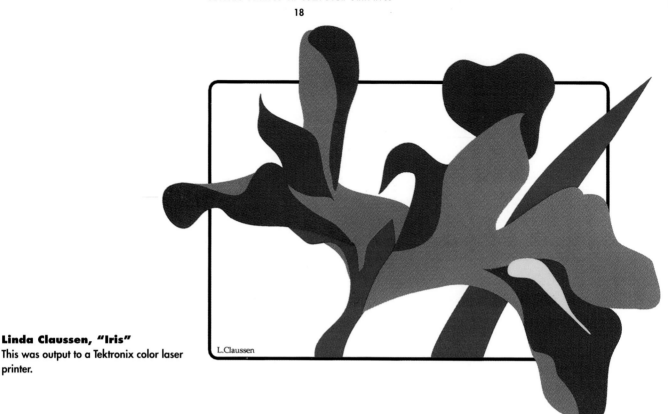

Linda Claussen, "Iris"
This was output to a Tektronix color laser printer.

L.Claussen

are twice as fast (33 megahertz) as my Mac IIfx. If I had started out with an IBM computer, I would likely have owned 286 and 386 machines and now be looking at a 486/33 megahertz machine.

Scrimping on a display screen and graphics card. If you intend to work in color and prepare large, detailed work, you'll go crazy chasing your drawings around on a tiny black-and-white screen. You should configure your entire computer system around your screen and the graphics board that controls it. Choosing better monitor technology is important, too. Your monitor should display color with sharpness and without distortion or flicker. It should also do a good job displaying type characters.

Graphics boards can feature some interesting and productive tools. Hardware pan and zoom controls allow fast magnification and panning, bypassing slower software-activated controls. Video input/output allows for importation of video images as well as image exportation back to video media. This feature is increasingly valuable if you plan to work with animation or multimedia production.

SHOPPING FOR THE RIGHT DISPLAY MONITOR
Save your money for a better color monitor.

Buying the best-quality monitor is difficult because there are so many choices. Furthermore, video electronics is a difficult technology for nonengineering types to understand. But this I know: When it comes to monitors, you get what you pay for.

Why are they so expensive? A color computer monitor is not exactly your ordinary television set. Computer monitors actually represent the most advanced engineering available in a CRT device. You wouldn't be happy with the screen resolution offered by your television.

In terms of display technologies, there are three types of monitors: analog, digital and multisynchronous (capable of reproducing both analog and digital signals of various frequencies). Analog signals bring you television—images from a videotape. Digital signals are those generated by a computer that processes information as numerical values. A multisynchronous monitor (also called a multiscan) can display both analog and digital signals.

A multiscan monitor can take advantage of a wide range of graphic standards (thus the name "multiscan"). If you want to hook a video capture board to your system so that you can import analog images into your computer and digitize them for computer graphics, a multiscan monitor is your best bet.

From a more practical standpoint, a multisynchronous monitor can run on virtually any computer. If you should change brands of computer, you can keep your screen. A multiscan monitor gives you a measure of flexibility but at a higher price.

Tom Nielson, "Red-Haired Woman"
Texas artist Nielson created this illustration on a PC with Micrografx Designer, a versatile, object-oriented graphics program for the IBM. His output was on a Tektronix printer.

COLOR GRAPHICS DISPLAY BOARDS

Your computer's ability to display color images is controlled by a circuit board located between your computer's CPU and monitor. A variety of boards, or cards, are available from your computer maker as well as third-party developers. Your computer is equipped with slots into which these boards can be easily installed.

In a one-bit display, the pixel is either on (white) or off (black). On a finer resolution display, patterns of on-and-off pixels can simulate gray halftones in a bit-map array. But to get good continuous tone grays, you must advance to gray scale.

Gray-scale display boards have four to eight bits-per-pixel shades of gray, which support up to 256 shades of gray. This environment is perfectly suited for gray scale images or black-and-white photo editing.

The most basic color board is the 8-bit card, supporting at the most 256 colors onscreen at one time. Each pixel receives eight bits of information to display a color.

The trend in computer color technology is 24-bit color. Each pixel contains 24 bits of color information and has the ability to represent 16.8 million colors onscreen simultaneously. While you may not believe that you'd ever use this much color, a 24-bit display card will give you continuous colors that blend smoothly without banding—critical to working with scanned color images, especially photographic images.

It isn't absolutely necessary to have a 24-bit graphics display card to continue to create spectacular graphics. Though I now have a 24-bit RasterOps card, I could probably pursue my design and illustration career just as well with an 8-bit graphics display card. However, to create truly accurate and

Jim Thompson, "Jim's Space Composition"
Jim's experience as an airbrush artist has served him well in his transition to creating computer graphics on a PC.

realistic images that display richness, depth, dimension and form, 256 colors is not enough. Higher resolution images demand an even greater number of colors onscreen to recreate subtle tonal variations. So, I probably wouldn't buy anything less than a 24-bit accelerated graphics card.

WHAT TO LOOK FOR WHEN MONITOR SHOPPING
Is the display sharp from edge to edge?
Examine the monitor's technical specifications—like frequency of the video band width. In a high-resolution monitor with a fast scan rate, a higher frequency is necessary to avoid horizontal blurring of pixels. In a group of comparable

computer monitors, band widths range from as low as 17 to as high as 200 megahertz. Monitors with low band widths of 17 megahertz are likely to be less sharp than ones with 200 megahertz band widths.
Does the screen seem to flicker or flutter when you move your eyes across it?
Display sharpness, image flutter or flicker is influenced by your monitor's vertical scan rate, sometimes referred to as a "frame rate." It refers to the number of times per second the screen redraws (50 hertz means the screen refreshes 50 times per second). Flicker is noticeable out of the corner of your eye and is fatiguing for your eyes after some hours. It is particularly noticeable on large

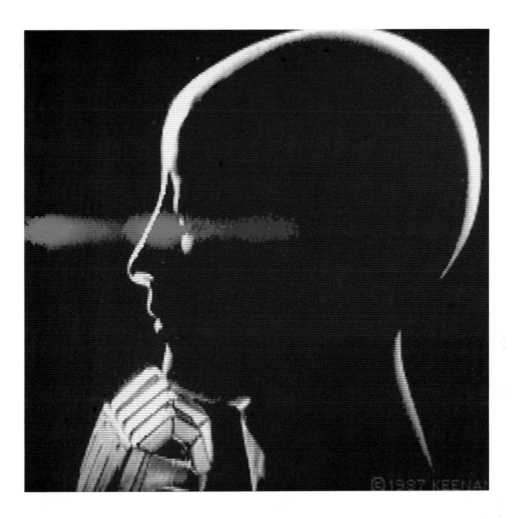

Larry Keenan, "Prism Profile"
Keenan used Digiview and DeluxePaint software on an Amiga to create this illustration.

screens. Choose a monitor with a vertical scan rate of at least 65 hertz. This will be fast enough to eliminate flicker on a large screen.

Does the image bow out at the sides or otherwise look distorted? And what are those glares and flares? The screen isn't flat enough. The faceplate is displaying the characteristics of a wide-angled lens. Image bowing may also be the result of "pincushioning," which could be corrected by adjustments to controls inside the monitor's case.

Does black type on a white background look like brown type against a gray or blue background? This monitor is probably not in registration, nor is it very bright. And it is probably using a cheaper conventional CRT technology like Delta or PIL (precision-in-line), which is what you might buy with an inexpensive monitor. Compare the monitor you're looking at to a Sony Trinitron, and you'll see better representation of black type on a white background. You'll see a brighter, flatter, mostly flicker-free display.

What is that ghost, or is it a shadow? And what are those stripes? Ghosts, stripes (horizontal shadows), and distortion are less evident on monitors with more powerful horizontal scan rates. This kind of quality is determined more by a particular monitor brand's technology than by price. A good test when looking for monitor flaws is to fill the screen with different-size characters of type and horizontal and vertical lines from edge to edge. Display as many regular weight type faces as possible and a variety of thin, straight lines. Do the lines bow? Do

Jason Challas, "Desert Walk"
This California artist uses a Targa still-video frame grabber board and Adobe Photoshop to combine and render his pieces.

SHOPPING FOR A COMPUTER OUTPUT DEVICE

A number of different printers are on the market. Several are laser printers, the devices made famous by desktop publishing. You will probably examine two types of laser printers: PostScript and non-PostScript laser printers. PostScript is a trade name of Adobe Systems. It has become the most popular output and page display language of desktop publishing.

PostScript is a complex language of numerical codes that links the drawing or type on your screen to a PostScript printing device. The PostScript code plots the outlines of the shapes you have drawn on your computer screen. If you have specified that the shapes be filled in, the program will tell the printer to do just that.

Some laser printers are non-PostScript, relying on other languages. There's nothing wrong with any of these languages but certain drawing and desktop publishing software and typefaces may only be compatible with PostScript printers. Some printers support a variety of machine languages, and that's good. If you work with material from a variety of sources and other computers, this would be advantageous.

In any event, PostScript has become the device language of choice.

If you want to draw free-form graphics, compose and manipulate type, and produce crisp, high-resolution quality, you will probably want to look at computers and software that work with PostScript.

THE COLOR PRINTER

When I prepared the first edition of this book, I longingly wrote about the availability of color printing technology. Quite frankly, I couldn't afford a color printer at the going price of $10,000-plus. Well, times change, prices drop, and the

the letters get fuzzy at the screen's edges? This is the best way I know of to test display quality.

STRATEGIES FOR GETTING YOUR GRAPHICS TO YOUR CLIENT
If you're a freelancer, should you look at an expensive color output device?

You could rely on service bureaus, and maybe buy an inexpensive fax modem for your computer—a little box connected directly to the computer that links you to a telephone line. This would allow you to send proofs of your work right off your screen to anyone who has a fax or similarly equipped computer. If your computer is equipped with a scanner, you can scan photos, contracts, price lists or even three-dimensional objects, and transmit that via your computer's fax modem.

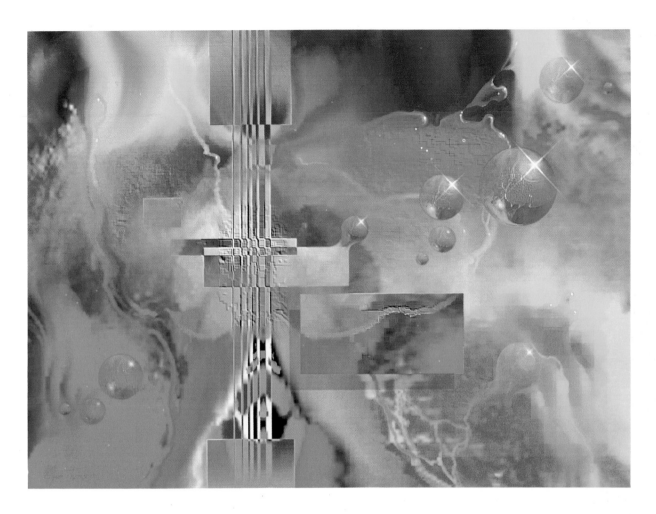

color printer I now have retails for less than $5,000. It's more than just a luxury in my graphic arts business—it's an absolute necessity.

In fact, when I talk to other artists who are looking at building a personal graphics computing system, I suggest half seriously to start with the best printer they can afford and work backward toward the best computer platform that would support that printer. A good color printer in the hands of a graphic artist is literally a money-making machine. You can make accurate color comps of your project, and, in several cases, I've actually used the final color printer output for final reproduction-quality art. My printer is a Tektronix Phaser II color wax transfer printer. It's built like a battleship and (knock on wood) has not given me an ounce of trouble.

There are inexpensive color ink-jet and Color Bubble-Jet (Canon) printers on the market that can give you excellent resolution for proofing purposes. On the other hand, if you can justify the cost of higher resolution printing, here are some technologies to consider:

Wax Transfer Printers: These use a ribbon of thin, transparent colored wax that is transferred to special paper. These printers produce adequate resolution with 300 dpi output, and are especially good for producing presentation transparencies. Paper prints are shiny and color-rich. Wax transfer printers

Jim Thompson, "Abstract #1"
Artist Jim Thompson worked with state-of-the-art PC technology to produce these stunning visuals. Jim outputs his creations to a film processor that's capable of producing large format as well as 35mm slides of his work.

James Dowlen, "Flower"
This illustration was created using Time Arts Lumena software on an Everex computer.

cost from $3,000 to $10,000. Consumables (wax transfer ribbons and coated paper) put print costs at approximately $1 per page.

Continuous Tone Die Sublimation Printers: These devices are similar to wax transfer printers but use dies that are coated on plastic film. As the paper passes a thermal head, the dies are changed from solid to gas, which is absorbed by special coated paper. This technology requires comparatively costly consumables, but it produces prints of incredible accuracy and brilliance. Each print can cost as much as $5. Kodak ($20,000 at this writing) and RasterOps ($12,000 at this writing) manufacture these printers.

Color Phase Change Printers: This technology uses environmentally friendly color wax crayons (cyan, magenta, yellow and black) that are melted and squirted onto plain paper at a surprisingly high resolution 300 dpi. Tektronix makes one of the best, delivering rich, Pantone-certified color. Because of the ease of maintenance and low cost of consumables (the printer uses plain paper of virtually any grade instead of coated stock), operating costs are comparatively low. The price for the printer (in the neighborhood of $10,000 at this writing) is pretty sobering, however, for the solo artist. The price would be more easily justified in a design firm.

Color Laser Printers: The deluxe model in this category is the Canon Color Laser Copier System. Of course you are looking at a $50,000-plus device. But for higher volume color printing requirements with output sizes up to tabloid (11-by-17-inch), such a machine would be useful to an advertising agency or graphic design studio.

High-Resolution Ink-Jet Technology: Originally designed to proof page layouts before committing to plate, this technology has been developed and modified by companies such as Scitex, the high-end prepress publication assembly system developer. In response to the request of computer graphics specialists for large-scale originals, some service bureaus now offer output as large as 4 feet wide on a variety of high-quality art papers. Photographers as well as artists find this creative output solution attractive, even at a per-copy price (large format, of course) of $150. These devices, including the Iris ink-jet printer, which delivers extremely high resolutions, start at $50,000. This puts them out of the reach of the average individual illustrator or design studio, but you may want to track down a bureau that offers this service if you do much large-scale work.

Computer graphics are being used in a variety of advanced design applications. This is a screen from an integrated painting, visual reference database, and computer-aided manufacturing package called ModaCAD. ModaCAD has developed a design program for the fashion industry that enhances the production process of getting a fashion design to finished garment. Classic fashions are in a CD-ROM-based image file that can be recalled by the designer to inspire a new creation. The resulting design can then be output to a plotter device, which creates a full-size pattern for garment fabrication. The program also allows the clothing designer to work effectively with patterns.

Louis Markoya, "Green Chrome Spider From Mars"
Markoya, who worked closely with Salvador Dali, produces fantastic illustrations with the Commodore Amiga and a variety of software. He combines ray tracing, scanned images and freehand paintings. He often uses Hamendel graphic software. Hamendel uses fractal geometry to create realistic three-dimensional objects and landscapes.

Some Alternative Solutions for Color Output:

Slides and service bureaus.

High-resolution color output devices are costly. However, if you live in an area where service bureaus can supply you with color output or litho-negative separations that can, in turn, produce color proofs, this strategy is a lower cost, short-term alternative.

Some computer artists don't use printers at all but output their images to photographic transparency equipment, some of which use standard 35mm cameras and slide film. Don't confuse these with color printers that can be loaded with overhead transparency film for presentation graphics. The equipment that produces images directly on 35mm film are precision devices designed to accurately reproduce the color images and resolution of your computer image.

The artists who produce graphics for video productions don't usually need hard copies of their work since their art is captured, stored and displayed on videotape.

Output of full-color raster-based and vector images to slides has obvious advantages. However, many color drawing and painting programs, designed to allow artists to publish their graphics, allow for output directly to color separation negatives via devices like the Linotronic. The negatives can then be used to produce four-color or spot-color proofs and ultimately laysheets for burning plates in the lithographic process.

OF MICE AND ARTISTS
Alternative input devices.

The most popular user-interface for screen rendering is the mouse. Here's what to look for when purchasing an accessory mouse for your computer.

Most mice are mechanical contrivances. The ball, as it moves about on the pad, rolls little wheels inside the mouse's housing. This mechanism allows you to navigate the cursor across the screen in synchronous movements.

For drawing purposes, I prefer an optical mouse. This is a non-mechanical variety that uses a beam of light (instead of a ball) on a reflective pad. This provides me with smooth action and precise control over the computer pro-gram's drawing tools.

Summagraphics Corporation offers an electronic tablet, which uses a sleek electronic pen, for use with a Macintosh. The pen offers more continuity and tactile feel than a mouse. The Kurta Tablet is a variation on the electronic tablet concept. It can be configured with two different pointing devices: a pen or an improved mouse

One of the most important advances in how I paint and draw on the computer is the pressure-sensitive tablet. I had learned to draw pretty well using the mouse, but I missed the ability to make natural strokes, thin to thick and thick to thin, so to speak. Pressing harder on a mouse will only break the mouse.

Jim Thompson, "Ribbons and Bubbles"
Created using Time Arts Lumena software on an IBM-AT.

Nancy J. Freeman, "Woodland Scene"
This illustration was made on an Amiga and output to a Hewlett Packard Paint-Jet printer.

A pressure-sensitive tablet is equipped with a cordless pen that performs all of the Mac's normal mouse functions. However, in a graphics application, the stylus performs like a traditional rendering device. Changing the pressure of the stylus on the tablet changes the quality or character of the line; for example, pressing harder can produce a broader line, with the stylus behaving almost like a paintbrush or quill pen.

This pressure-sensitive response is produced through an ultra-fine grid of wires embedded in the tablet's surface, which emits and receives electromagnetic signals in microseconds. The pen acts as a transmission device that sends a radio signal through a battery-powered circuit or, in the case of the Wacom stylus, through a patented coil-and-capacitor resonant circuit, which stores and reemits electromagnetic energy. As the pen touches the tablet, the coordinate data are continually transmitted through the serial port to the CPU. At this writing, three pressure-sensitive tablets are available: the Wacom Digitizing Tablet, CalComp's Drawing Board II, and the Kurta XGT pressure-sensitive tablet.

A growing number of software companies offer drivers or utility software designed to be used with pressure-sensitive tablets. Many drawing and painting programs in both the Mac and IBM environment have tools that let you benefit from pressure sensitivity, including Aldus FreeHand, Aldus Super-Paint, Fractal Design Painter, Oasis, Studio/32 and Lumena. In Aldus FreeHand, for example, you can produce editable shapes that take on the characteristics of lines of variable thickness. Altsys Fontographer 3.5 for the Mac has a calligraphy tool that uses pressure sensitivity to allow you to simulate roughly 90 percent of all calligraphic strokes. Many image-editing programs such as Adobe PhotoShop, ColorStudio and Pixo-Foto have also incorporated this new feature.

I use the Wacom tablet because I prefer the feel and flexibility of the stylus. It's lightweight and easy to use even when working for a long time. Drawing Board II, on the other hand, is one-third less expensive and has several convenience features, such as a tracing aid, not available on the Wacom tablet. Unless those features and a lower price are absolutely critical,

Louis Markoya, "Watching Angel"
Created using Amiga.

I'd still recommend the Wacom tablet for quality and comfort.

SCANNERS

One of the most difficult computer accessories to shop for is the right scanner. The reason: So many are on the market! Scanners are simply digitizers. They allow you to get a photo, drawing or even three-dimensional object into your computer to be used in a document or manipulated in your drawing and painting program.

For you to manipulate any photographic image on a computer, it must be digitized. The photograph that you wish to translate into your computer is an analog image. You must convert your analog picture into a digital one—a "pixelmap"— to work with it on your computer.

The image's color(s) and contrast values are recorded by the scanner's head as it passes over the surface of the image. The scanner actually measures a photograph's color values and converts them into binary code, which is understood by your computer. The binary code sends hue, saturation and brightness control as well as formatting information and commands specific to the software used to facilitate the scan.

The binary code is interpreted by your computer imaging software, which works in concert with your computer's graphic display card to paint the pixelmap on your screen. This pixelmap can then be stored on a disk or other media for retrieval and display. Your image-editing software provides

James Dowlen, "Dragon Screen"
This illustration was used for the packaging of a PC-based graphic arts software program capable of three-dimensional modeling.

you with tools to manipulate those pixels on the pixelmap.

Scanner companies distribute their own software so you can manipulate your scanned images in a variety of ways—for example, overdrawing and painting or enhancing contrast and brightness. The software usually provides a number of graphics tools (pencils, paintbrushes, spray cans) to modify your scanned image. The software also enables you to prepare your graphic for exportation in a number of different file formats, such as TIFF (Tag Image File Format), EPS (Encapsulated PostScript), MacPaint, PICT (draw) and a few other configurations. This allows your image to be compatible with a number of other programs, like page layout software, which receive graphics.

So when you evaluate scanners, cut right to the scanners' software and ask these questions:
• How many export formats do they support?
• Are the manipulation tools easy or cumbersome to learn?
• Does the program provide a truly comfortable user interface for you?

One more useful function of a scanner should not be overlooked: Optical Character Reading (OCR). With variously priced software, your scanner can read documents into your word-processing program for editing and manipulation. Since I am also in the publishing business, this extra function makes my scanner a worthwhile investment.

There are sheet-fed scanners, flatbed scanners (which can do pages out of books), copy-stand scanners that can do three-dimensional objects, hand-held scanners (a cheaper way to have scanning capabilities) and color scanners.

If color is not an option on your system or within your budget, a gray-scale scanner is splendid for digitizing photographs and other images. I publish a black-and-white newspaper in addition to my color work. My newspaper workstation has a complete gray-scale setup—8-bit gray-scale monitor, 8-bit Apple gray-scale scanner—that I use with Adobe Photoshop image-editing software.

If you intend to integrate photos into publishing projects, you will need a scanner that can capture an adequate number of gray levels. Scanners can offer anything from 16 to 256 levels of gray. My only advice is to look at a gray-scale scanner that can capture at least 64 levels of gray. The more levels of gray your scanner can transcribe, the better your scans will look. But there is a down side. High-resolution scanned images are memory hogs. An 8-by-10-inch photograph scanned in gray scale can take up more than a megabyte of memory!

COLOR SCANNERS

Color scanners range from hand-held scanners to desktop drum scanners that come close to the color reproduction of the large drum scanners used by color separators. Hand-held and desktop flatbed color scanners can handle flat mediums such as photographs or renderings on paper. Most desktop scanners work with variable resolutions between 72 and 300 dpi, although some of the more expensive models scan up to 600 dpi, with 24 bits of color information.

If you work a lot with transparencies (anywhere between 4-by-5- to 8-by-10-inches), you won't be able to use a standard

flatbed scanner. Film allows light to shine through, requiring a mirror attachment of some sort to shine light back into the scanner. Some of the more expensive flatbed scanners offer mirror options, but most lower-priced desktop models don't.

If your original artwork is most often 35mm slides, or if you need to create high-resolution scans on the desktop, consider getting a slide scanner. These range from $6,000 to $30,000 in price, depending on the types of film accepted and the output resolution. BarneyScan and Nikon both make high-end scanners with reputations for good-quality output as well as scanners that have midrange prices and medium level quality. You can't scan 35mm slides on a flatbed scanner; the results are awful.

For critical pre-press operations, you'll need to work with dedicated pre-press systems. The major players in this market are Scitex, Hell and Crossfield. Dedicated desktop scanner systems, such as the

Peter McCormick, "Summer Days"
Created in Fractal Design Painter for Windows on the PC.

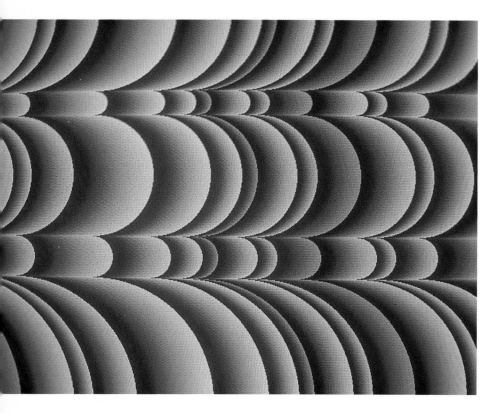

Allen Cosgrove, "Sculptural Scallops"
Cosgrove uses an Apple IIe and graphics software that he wrote himself . He generates images with a Vectrix 384A Color Graphics Processor and an analog RGB color display.

Optronics ColorGetter, are appearing and deliver pre-press quality source scans. When coupled with a calibrated monitor and well-maintained imagesetter, these units can be used as part of a viable high-end Mac-based color separation system. Unfortunately, dedicated desktop scanners tend to retail for $30,000 to $60,000, putting them out of reach for any but large, well-financed design studios and advertising agencies.

A number of companies are releasing reasonably good, low-priced desktop color scanners ($1,200 to $2,500). I have found that the best scanners for the money for the computer artist are desktop flatbed scanners that can scan 300 to 600 dpi.

ASSEMBLING YOUR COLLECTION OF GRAPHIC ARTS SOFTWARE

What follows is a recommendation of the types of graphic software

you should consider. You will need to choose:

A drafting program that allows you to create and manipulate high-resolution shapes, lines and type elements. The best, most flexible drafting programs for microcomputers use a high-resolution machine language that addresses an output device like a laser printer. Drafting programs produce what is termed object-oriented graphics on your computer that are "vector" graphics, meaning they are shapes defined by line, position, shape and fill pattern. Drafting programs have built-in precision drawing tools, which allow you to create precise and smooth curves and shapes. Drafting programs allow for large drawings—even to the size of a billboard. Although they don't handle curves as well as PostScript programs, they're great for charts, graphs and diagrams.

A PostScript drawing program that has all the features of a drafting program but with additional flexibility. You can create changeable shapes made up of a complex assemblage of contiguous lines and curves. Plus, a good program using PostScript device language has an auto-trace feature. You can import a bit-map graphic, like a scan, and turn it into a vector-based PostScript graphic for high-resolution conversion and laser printer output.

A painting program that not only has all of the flexible features you are looking for, but one that has a good, intuitive user interface. Painting programs create "raster-based" graphics composed of bit-maps. A distinct gridmap is used in the rendering process, and you will most often work at the "pixel level," that is, you will work with picture elements created on the grid.

A combination drafting/painting program that features both drafting

and painting tools. The program is actually composed of two different applications running in tandem, or more appropriately, layers, on the same screen. Two of the best examples in the Macintosh world are SuperPaint (Aldus) and Canvas (Deneba Software). These programs actually combine vector and raster-based image layers, providing the artist with the spontaneity and flexibility of painting tools and the crispness of object-oriented lines and shapes. This software approach has had its place in the evolution of computer graphics programs. And as high-resolution paint programs come on the scene, they will alleviate the need for such program sandwiches.

An image-editing program that is designed to be used with a scanning device to make your computer a photo darkroom and retouching studio. These programs can combine and manipulate scanned images. You can use this powerful software for more than digitizing ordinary photos. Creative artists use their scanners to capture anything from hand-rendered and three-dimensional images to pieces of cloth and colorful tiles. I frequently capture three-dimensional images with a video camera, plug the camera into the graphics display card on my computer, and digitize frames of video in full color. I can then manipulate these images and combine them with others to create visual compositions.

A collection of type faces, of which there are hundreds available for your computer. PostScript fonts are extremely popular with microcomputer users. Other electronic type formats, include Compu-

Gary Olsen, "Three Seagulls"
This illustration was prepared using PixelPaint on a Macintosh and output to a Tektronix color laser printer.

Jim Pollock, "Bison"
This South Dakota artist creates Western motifs on a Macintosh using MacPaint.

graphic, Bitstream and Apple's TrueType, to mention three. PostScript faces, marketed by PostScript's originator, Adobe Systems, have established themselves as the high-quality standard for microcomputer applications.

A REMARKABLE HYBRID COLOR COMPUTER
Computer graphics isn't all Macintoshes and IBMs.
Commodore's Amiga has carved itself an important niche as the hippest of all color computers. In progressive design, video production and animation studios around the country and in Europe, you will likely find Commodore Amigas. Some years ago, when Macintosh was first introduced as the "new generation of computing," Commodore, a leader in powerful com-

puters that you could actually buy at a discount store, introduced the Amiga. Unfortunately, a lack of focus and a clear market, complicated by a lack of software support in the early stages, caused Amiga to roll slowly out of its starting gate.

Since its introduction in 1985, the Amiga has earned a loyal following among graphic designers, but even more devotion among those who consider themselves computer fine artists. It wasn't just a lower price that attracted these people. It was Amiga's functionality and powerful color controls. Amiga's standard high-resolution graphic display and a motherboard that generates 4,096 colors without a separate and expensive color board is a pretty good deal.

Some fairly sophisticated and comparatively low-cost software is

1.
"With FreeHand's new pressure sensitive drawing tool, my WACOM tablet allows me to create completely enclosed paths with a single stroke. The tool mimicks perfectly a variable line brush stroke."

2.
"Since we're in FreeHand, editing the path is no problem. A pull here, a tug there."

3.
"Another WACOM stroke for the wing accent."

4.
"The head was comprised of three strokes. The precision of the WACOM stylus makes precise manipulation of vector points a breeze."

available for the Amiga, including advanced drawing and painting programs, animation, three dimension, fractals, ray tracing and even desktop video production tools.

Gary Olsen, "S.S. Wacom"
This piece was prepared using FreeHand and the Wacom pressure-sensitive tablet. It was output from a Techtronix Color Phase III printer that uses ink-jet technology.

I was commissioned to submit a logo concept for a housing and country club development in Florida. The original design concept of the "cat eyes" against a solid background was created by another designer. I was asked to expand on the original motif. The client wanted a little more identity with the cat, so I experimented with some silhouettes.

However, I really didn't know what type of cat the original artist was thinking about when he rendered the eyes. I asked my client, and he didn't know either.

Was it a mountain lion? A bobcat? Both kinds of cats can be found in Florida, so I decided to give my client some choices. Working with a computer, choices are extremely easy to create.

I first went to the encyclopedia, looked up cats, and found great reference pictures. I began drawing a loose outline of a cat on my Macintosh in FullPaint, a wonderfully simple monochrome paint program. When I discovered my first drawing resembled a house cat rather than a wildcat, I began to make some modifications.

1. I combined the scanned image of the client's "cat eyes" motif and my loosely painted cat in my monochrome paint program. However, the feline looks too much like a house cat. I could modify it—stretch it, draw connecting lines, fill in the gaps with a brush or paint bucket, and trim the ears so that they appear to lay back. The most important tools are the marquee and lasso.

YOUR PAINTING TOOLS:

Direct rendering tools: pencil, paint bucket, eraser, and paintbrush.

Object manipulation and movement tools: The lasso is for moving contiguous groups of black pixels only; the marquee is for moving both black and surrounding white pixels within the specific area of the marquee's rectangle. Irregularly shaped areas of your illustration can be selected by the lasso and copied, pasted, or moved about on the screen. Areas of your painting selected by the marquee are rectangular. They can be duplicated and moved, but also stretched, shrunk, flipped, reversed, and so on.

Auto-tracing tool: More painting programs are offering this feature. It can create a PostScript or Quickdraw outline of a bit-map graphic for export to a drawing program and subsequent output on a high-resolution printing device.

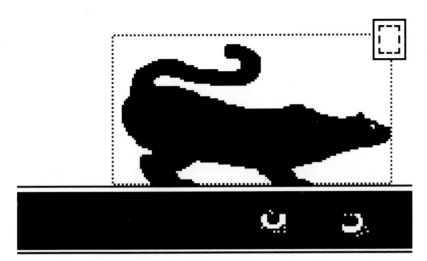

2. The eraser is used to change the shape of the head to be more pantherlike. The body of the cat is stretched to accentuate the musculature of a large panther. There are two ways to stretch the cat's body. One way is to use the marquee box, select the image and just stretch it. However, this might expand the pixels, making the outline more jagged. There is a better way.

3. The better way to elongate the cat is to cut it in half with the marquee tool, slide one section over, and connect the halves with the pencil or brush. Also, the paintbrush can be used to beef up the legs. That upturned tail has got to go. You can erase it. Paint a better tail off to the side, lasso it and drag it to the exact place you want it.

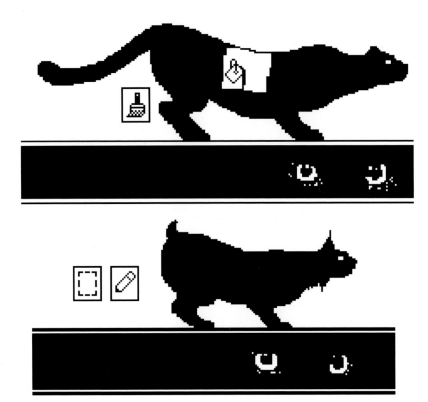

4. The tail on this panther is perfect. It no longer gives him away if he is stalking something or preparing to pounce. The paintbrush was used to draw the optional tail, and the lasso was used to select and drag it into place. The eraser, of course, eliminated the old tail and helped refine the cat's musculature. The thought occurred to me that maybe the client would like to see a bobcat rather than a panther. By selecting the cat with the marquee tool and compressing it, the feline indeed resembled a lynx or bobcat. A few touches with the pencil (longer ears and a boxlike head) and the eraser (the tail is now bobbed) and you have another version of the cat to show the client.

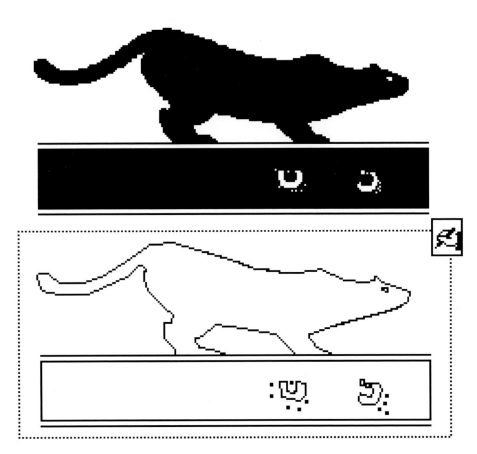

5. The client saw the different versions of the cat, and settled on the panther. The next step was to turn the rough bit-mapped graphic into a smooth PostScript piece of line art. The bottom image is a screen snapshot of the freshly auto-traced line work. These closed line paths are easily filled with solid color. With a PostScript line, you have a much more editable graphic. You can tug lines into new positions and finish details around the eyes. Adobe Illustrator (Mac and PC versions), Micrografx Designer (PC) and Aldus Free-Hand (Mac) have excellent auto-tracing tools that can handle a variety of imported bit-map renderings you create in other programs.

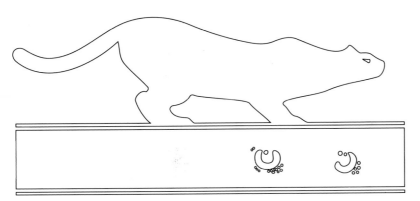

6. Here's an example of a PostScript line conversion in Adobe's Illustrator program. Illustrator, like most popular PostScript drawing packages, allows you to import the image into its program environment where you can tackle the graphic with PostScript's auto-tracing tool. Your image now becomes smoother, the lines more precisely rendered. Also, you can specify the fill colors (in this case, black).

7. The finished product with the recommended logotype in place. Note that I've specified yellow fills on the white portion of the eyes. The graphic doesn't exactly need color to have impact, but this spare amount to give the the entire graphic some presence is not a bad idea.

WILDCAT RUN

I developed this logo for a communications consultant and friend, Joe Williams. In fact, I taught a publication design workshop with him as part of his "Dialogue in the Desert" series. Among the students' projects in my workshop was the creation of an alumni newsletter. We needed a unique design to capture the spirit of our week-long workshop experience at a beautiful desert resort in Wickenburg, Arizona.

Every morning we awakened to the sounds of desert quail. These birds became a symbol of our experience, so we wanted to somehow incorporate them in our newsletter's banner. The entire graphic was prepared in MacDraw. I have included the icons that represent the onscreen tools this object-oriented drafting program uses to render a letter, ellipse, freehand shape or line.

Some programs like Aldus Free-Hand for the Mac and PC have a freehand shape tool that is designed for use with pressure-sensitive tablets. I utilized this tool for the quick rendering of the quail. Other programs like Adobe Illustrator may have a command that lets you turn type into outlines and manipulate it as shown here. Both FreeHand and Illustrator, as well as many other PostScript rendering programs, now have extended page-layout capabilities. This means you can now create a complex layout like this without ever leaving your rendering program.

D

1. With your font tool, type a large letter D. Make it boldface and, if possible, 140 points. It should be large enough to contain our key logo element—a white silhouette of a quail.

2. With your ellipse or oval tool, create an oval.

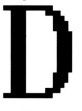

3. To resize or change the characteristics of the oval to measure the same height as the D, use your select tool. Once the oval is selected, pushing and pulling on the grabbers will manipulate the shape.

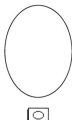

4. After you have positioned the oval over the letter D, try to fine-tune the size. Don't worry about those triangles. You'll take care of them later. For now, assign a black fill to the oval with the fill command.

YOUR DRAFTING TOOLS:

Tools found in typical PostScript Drawing or Drafting Programs.

Font tool: One of the best features of PostScript drawing and drafting programs is the font tool. It enables you to integrate smooth, professional looking text in your compositions.

Rendering tools: The freehand line tool and the straight line tool. Often there are separate horizontal and angle line tools. Some PostScript drawing and drafting programs also feature a bezier curve tool.

Shape tools: The oval or ellipse tool, rectangle tool, and trapezoid tool enable you to draw specific shapes quickly and easily. The trapezoid tool allows you to make multi-sided shapes. Just clicking your mouse button at whatever screen locations you choose defines the shape. The rounded rectangle tool does exactly what its name implies. Corner radii are adjustable.

Select tools: To select a shape or element you have already drawn on the screen, use the arrow tool and click on the element you wish to move, delete, change, or manipulate. The marquee tool allows you to select more than one object at a time for movement, deletion, copying, and pasting.

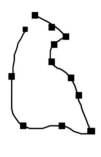

5. With the freehand tool, draw an approximate rendering of the quail's body. Don't worry about accuracy. You can tug the lines into a precise shape by repositioning the grabbers.

6. Freehand the top knot, then, using the select tool, drag it over to the rest of the figure. The select tool can reselect any aspect of the drawing elements for fine-tuning as well as movement. The quail is a shape now, so specify the fill. It should be white. Drag it on top of the D/oval elements drawn previously.

7. The straight line tool will help us render the quail's leg. The thickness and color of the line is controlled in the line attributes menu of our drawing program. In this case, the color of the line is white.

IALOGUE

8. Now you can take care of those triangles of white. They can be patched with black triangles drawn with the trapezoid tool. Draw them off to the side and drag them into position. This is a good time to print out your graphic once again to check that "what you are seeing is what your are getting" (WYSIWYG). Make any adjustments before advancing to the next step.

9. Use the marquee tool and select all elements of your graphic. Select "Group" from your Arrange or Objects menu. This will glue all of the elements together in one solid unit that can be easily resized (or reshaped vertically or horizontally). As a solid unit, you can move the graphic about on the screen without leaving little bits behind.

10. Based on what you have learned so far, can you identify the tools it required to create the graphic elements above? This is the part of the graphic lesson that allows your own creative juices to flow. If you can improve on the banner below, wonderful! To get your started, remember the size of the original D? If you haven't resized it, it's probably still 140 points. That's what the E should be above. The rest of the letters should be around 100 points or whatever looks best. "In the Desert" is set at perhaps 24 points and reversed against the black rounded corner rectangle.

PUBLISHED BY STUDENTS OF THE JOE WILLIAMS COMMUNICATIONS WORKSHOPS

PAINTING AND DRAWING

. . . .

**The difference between preparing object-oriented graphics,
drafting graphics, PostScript drawings
and bit-mapped paint graphics.**

There are now four classifications of graphic programs for microcomputers, and it's important to understand the features that distinguish each.

Paint programs create raster bit-mapped images. Bit-maps are simply a matrix of dots or pixels. The resolution of your image corresponds to the resolution of your computer's screen. Basically, the artist moves a pointing device across the screen, turning pixels on or off. In color programs, each pixel contains closely spaced red, green and blue dots that can be varied in intensity to synthesize a spectrum of continuous tone and colors.

Paint programs contain onscreen tools (icons) that mimic traditional drawing and painting tools—a pencil, brushes, pens and a paint-spraying device. You can even create paint spatter effects or, with a "smear tool," blend one "wet" color into another. The artist can express herself freely and spontaneously in a paint program.

Type is handled differently in a paint program than it is in drafting

. . . .

Max Seabaugh, "Texas"
An unpublished illustration using Adobe
Illustrator on a Macintosh.

or PostScript drawing programs. In most simple paint programs, type elements are low-resolution bit-maps. Drafting and PostScript programs, on the other hand, render smoothly executed type faces.

Drafting programs create vector images. The artist plots vectors (points) that define precise lines and geometric shapes (rectangles, ellipses, Bézier curves and trapezoids). These vector images are actually mathematically computed formulas called algorithms—the mathematical formulas that form the basis of all object-oriented drawing programs. Algorithms are specific instructions that define a process and generate a result in a finite number of steps. There are algorithms that can create a perfect circle, square, rectangle or any other closed geometric shape. There are algorithms that calculate a Bézier curve, a straight line, a line of any thickness, and a pattern or color.

The results of these algorithmic equations are called objects. Drafted shapes can be filled with colors, patterns or shades of gray.

PostScript drawing programs are like drafting programs, but much more flexible. PostScript is a specific device language developed by Adobe Systems. Device language (or machine

language) is the computer code that drives output devices such as a laser printer, imagesetter or film processor.

PostScript printer output always exceeds your screen resolution. PostScript drawing programs are designed to drive high-resolution output devices, which actually do all the labor of drawing smooth lines, crisp and clean type, and continuous shades of color or gray.

In a PostScript drawing program, colors and shades are called "fills." Fills can be solid and continuous tone, radial, or even graduated fills of two or more colors (depending on the sophistication of the program and power of the computer). Fills can also contain patterns.

Combination drawing and painting programs create both raster bit-mapped and vector-based lines and shapes. One of the pioneering programs in this category is SuperPaint from Silicon Beach Software (a subsidiary of Aldus) for the Macintosh, a relatively inexpensive but powerful program that's extremely easy to use. Another excellent program that combines object-oriented drawing with bit-map painting is Canvas by Deneba Software of Miami, Florida. Most every incarnation since has been based on the same metaphor. Draw and paint elements are executed on their own

Jim Thompson, "Spheres and Checkers"
This illustration was made using Time Arts Lumena software on an IBM-AT.

separate layers or overlays. Basically, SuperPaint is two programs in one. Combination drawing and painting programs are ideal for combining paint images with high-resolution type.

High-resolution paint programs create high-resolution bit-maps for high-definition display and publishing quality output devices. These programs have migrated down from high-priced, dedicated platforms to the more affordable microcomputer class.

A steady improvement in high-resolution displays, faster and more powerful microcomputers, and larger and more efficient data storage devices encourages software developers to design programs capable of using this power. The goal of developers has long been to create paint programs capable of producing high-quality, high-resolution continuous tone images to compete with traditionally produced, publishing quality graphics.

Painting, drafting and drawing are distinctly different functions and have a different feel on a microcomputer, at least at this stage of technological development. The main differences are not just in how the programs perform or the type of graphics they produce. The difference that really matters to a graphic designer is the resolution of their output. Traditionally, raster graphics, prepared in a paint program, have contained lower resolution than vector graphics prepared with a drawing or drafting program. But this is changing as computers and software become more powerful.

THE DIFFERENCE IN FEEL

An artist can usually plunge right into a painting program, making easily correctable mistakes as a composition takes shape. But with a drawing program, the artist must plan more and develop a strategy. Working with Bézier curves, linking object-oriented lines, and grouping or joining shapes to form a single shape is initially difficult work for the novice. However, the results are usually stunning. What would take the designer hours to draw with French curves, technical pens, and straight edges, takes much less time in a computer drawing package. What the designer lost in initial prep time is gained with the ability to change elements in the drawing quickly, easily, and at any time—a task that can be impossible using traditional drawing tools.

WORKING IN ONE LAYER OR MULTILAYERS

Another thing that distinguishes painting programs from drawing and drafting applications is the fact that drawing is a multilayer environment and painting is basically a one-layer environment. There is an exception to this. Hybrid painting and drafting programs (such as SuperPaint and Canvas) provide you with both painting and drafting tools in one application. Paint tools are on one transparent layer and drawing tools are on another layer.

James Dowlen, "Robosport"
Dowlen has an amazing facility with both photo manipulation and three-dimensional rendering applications.

Most paint programs are "one-layer" programs. Every time you change or add something to your painting, it changes that graphic permanently, altering whatever you had painted previously. The exception to this is if your computer program has an "undo" command.

In drafting and PostScript drawing programs, every small thing you add to your drawing is a separate element. These programs treat each element as if it were drawn on a separate sheet of clear plastic and laid atop the previous elements you've drawn. All previous elements remain unchanged.

Drafting and drawing programs, therefore, provide the artist with complete graphic control. At virtually any time, the artist can descend through the layers of a drawing, pick out an offending line, change or modify it in some way, and that's it. Note, though, that picking through several layers of elements in a small and complex drawing can be frustrating. More sophisticated programs provide you with layer control, allowing you to isolate previously drawn elements.

POSTSCRIPT DRAWING PROGRAMS
Increasing your latitude.

In a drafting program, you can draw a rectangle, polygon, ellipse, Bézier curve or straight line. Each of these items can be resized, but they cannot be cut apart and combined with one another to form a more complex shape.

In a PostScript drawing program, you also possess tools that can render rectangles, ellipses, Bézier curves and straight lines. However, you also have a powerful freehand drawing tool that can render straight lines and Bézier curves in a series. You have the ability to create extremely complex shapes. The vector points, which connect the lines that form a shape, can be cut apart and rejoined to other points, thereby making your shape even more complex. The lines can be manipulated and curved to conform to any path you choose.

PAINT PROGRAM ADVANTAGES:
• They can be infinitely more flexible than drafting and PostScript drawing programs in managing color, line weight and variation, freehand shapes and customized fill patterns.
• They have several more tools and special effects.
• They make better and more spontaneous sketchbooks for rapid rendering of ideas.
• It's easier to draw irregular shapes and lines.
• There's a flatter learning curve in the artist's quest toward proficiency.

PAINT PROGRAM DISADVANTAGES:
• It's more difficult to modify a graphic prepared in a paint program than one created in a drawing program. With paintings, you have to "push pixels" to change your composition, and it can be quite tedious. Manipulating color is also more difficult.

L. Claussen

Linda Claussen, "Iris in SuperPaint"
Claussen uses various low-resolution pixeled patterns to create form in this flower. She used SuperPaint on a Macintosh.

Sibyl Moss, "Too Rad for Mom and Dad"
This T-shirt illustration was created using Adobe Illustrator on a Macintosh.

• The characteristics and features that make today's paint programs so powerful and flexible tend to make rendering a slower process compared to working in object-oriented drawing programs. Even with practice in painting programs, a designer can likely prepare an assignment faster in Adobe Illustrator than in PixelPaint or Fractal Design Painter. Painting applications need lots of computer power and speed to run, so productivity might be a problem in a paint program environment.

• Font manipulation is more difficult in a paint program than in a PostScript drawing program. You can see the disadvantages of preparing fonts in a paint program as you experiment with various applications. In most paint programs, I hardly ever use the font tools. That's too bad, actually, since a good paint program creates some excellent fonts, and when printed through a high-resolution output device, they are quite acceptable. High-resolution painting programs feature anti-aliasing, which smooths the letters' jaggy edges.

DRAFTING AND DRAWING PROGRAM ADVANTAGES:

• They use high-resolution output languages for precisely drawn and smooth lines.

• They produce smooth, high-resolution type faces, which can be manipulated in several interesting ways.

• Output can be tailored to specific commercial printer technology (though many high-resolution paint programs now include this feature). For drawing and drafting programs, output can take the form of spot-color or four-color separations.

• Changes to finished graphics can be made more readily since vector and PostScript graphics never lose their element handling tools (for example, grabbers, manipulators, handles). Selecting (clicking on) the element reveals these grabbers, which can then be manipulated to change the shape and characteristic of the line or, in the case of a closed shape, the style of fill pattern, color, tint or gray halftone pattern.

• Fill colors can be created using the RGB or CMYK process color models or can include widely accepted Pantone colors (in PostScript programs like Aldus FreeHand, Adobe Illustrator, Micrografx Designer or CorelDRAW).

DRAFTING AND DRAWING PROGRAM DISADVANTAGES:

• They require more training, practice and planning to get started because of all the layers that are created with every element added to the graphic. It can be difficult navigating through the layers to change one line or element.

• There is a lack of spontaneity or freedom in executing a PostScript or object-oriented drawing. However, you can make a drawing look spontaneous and painterly with practice and planning.

GETTING AROUND

Be advised that proper file formatting is important for graphics you plan to place in another software program. Avoid a lot of experimentation by consulting your software manual. It will tell you the formats that it supports for importation and exportation.

If you save a file in an incompatible or improper file format, your graphic will not display or

The birth of a breaking news graphic

While the Mac is now integrated into many phases of newspaper production, its most visible benefit is the ability to create instant information graphics for breaking news.

1. A graphic artist gets a middle-of-the-night phone call. The paper needs an infographic for a late-breaking story.

2. The editor fills the artist in on the details.

3. The artist rushes to the scene of the story to take photos and draw sketches.

4. Sketches in hand, the artist races against the clock to do a rough.

5. The editor takes the rough to the editorial budget meeting for final approval.

6. As the artist waits for approval, he begins to render the rough on the Mac.

7. The editor returns from the meeting with final changes and writes copy to accompany graphic.

8. The copy editor makes final changes to copy; final is sent to typesetter.

Lest we forget...

Mother's day is a time to remember all the things mom has done for us. Were it not for her caring and guidance, we could all wind up socially unacceptable slobs. Take for example the lessons we learned at the dinner table, a classic site for bad manners.

BAD TIMING: Neighborhood ball game always seems to end ten minutes after official dinner time.

HATS OFF to all moms on this special day, especially at the dinner table.

TALKING with your mouth full can produce hazardous waste.

FOOD IN CHEEKS: A habit we probably picked up from our friend, the squirrel.

FREE HAND furtively poised to make the infamous "boarding house reach."

IT'S OKAY to eat some food with your hands, but mashed potatoes are out.

MANY GREAT sculptors got their start at the dinner table. Here is a "work in progress."

ELBOWS ON THE TABLE: The classic mealtime faux pas. You're probably doing it right now.

KIDS ARE always finding clever ways to discard unwanted vegetables. How many can you think of?

NOTHING LIKE fine literature to enhance one's dining pleasure. Is that a Kafka novel?

THE OLD "feed the meatloaf to the dog" trick. Often passed off as an act of kindness.

NAPKIN: Size 12, denim blue. Also used as a hand towel and for junk storage.

Michael Gilmore, "Bad Habits"
(Above) Created for a newspaper feature story in the *Sun News,* Myrtle Beach, South Carolina. Gilmore used FreeHand on a Macintosh.

Jeff Goertzen, untitled
(Left) This illustration for *MacWeek* on the making of a breaking news graphic was created using FreeHand on a Macintosh. Goertzen is an illustrator for the *Orange County Register,* Orange County, California.

Jim Thompson, "Soap"
An excellent example of how the computer can render objects that would be extremely difficult to create with more traditional mediums. This was created using Time Arts Lumena software on an IBM-AT.

print correctly from the destination program. Here are the file formats explained:

TIFF (Tag Image File Format): This common bit-map save is the one most often used by scanning software. In a desktop publishing application, any scanned line art or gray-scale halftone can be saved as a TIFF and opened in another program such as a paint application (if you plan on modifying it) or a page-layout program like PageMaker, QuarkXPress or Ventura Publisher. TIFF files are formatted for high-resolution output on PostScript devices. TIFF also supports color but I don't recommend saving color files as TIFF, especially for a piece that is to be professionally printed.

RIFF (Raster Image File Format): This is the PC-based counterpart of TIFF.

PICT/PICT 2: This is like a TIFF but it supports color bit-map images for applications such as Photoshop, PixelPaint and Fractal Design Painter.

EPS Files (Encapsulated PostScript Files, often written simply as EPSF): This format is best for saving and placing high-resolution color image files intended for page layout and ultimately commercial printing. These files are perhaps the largest, in terms of disk space, because they must contain the color separation information through to the output device. Color PICT files can be placed in page-layout programs, but they take up a lot of file space, and should be converted into EPS files for use in page assembly.

Amiga ILF/ILBN: These are the formats readable on the Amiga platform. If your service bureau cannot handle this format, import these files into Adobe Photoshop to convert them to other formats.

MacPaint: This format enables you to further manipulate your image in MacPaint or in similar simple, bit-map editing programs. If you prepare an image that is viewable on a Macintosh compatible notebook computer that features one-bit display, you would save your image in MacPaint format.

About Pre-Press and PostScript

For graphics destined to be published, drawing programs afford the high resolution necessary for professional-looking graphics. In fact, drawing packages like Aldus Free-Hand and Adobe Illustrator were among the first programs developed for the graphic designer who creates material expressly for publication. They contain special commands that enable you to output your work in spot-color or four-color separations, complete with registration marks and margin notes for the printer. Therefore, most microcomputer drawing programs support a PostScript, high-resolution output device like a laser printer.

PostScript, Adobe System's brand name for its page description language, is contained in most of today's popular output devices. Other page description languages exist, but PostScript is the most popular device language around.

Historically, PostScript has been considered slow in output speed because of the amount of code the program needs to produce its high-resolution images on a page. Adobe has steadily improved its product, however, and, at the same time, computers and printing devices have improved their ability to handle PostScript economically.

Choosing Appropriate Software
What will your final form be?

Program reviews are extremely helpful in the evaluation of often-

© 1989 G.J. Olsen

DIVE IOWA

expensive software programs. Microcomputers and their accompanying software are well covered by many computer publications. Software reviews are generally featured in magazines of this genre. You'll soon learn to look for criticisms such as "how well the program follows a (particular computer's) user interface." We frequently hear the expression "user interface" when discussing software features. This refers to the visual and physical attributes of the program — its tools, text and graphics handling characteristics. If a program is easy to learn, has a slight

Gary Olsen, "Divers From Iowa"

This graphic was used both as a poster and a design for a T-shirt and visor. FreeHand produces spot- or process-color separations of graphics. Simply issue the spot-color print command to a laser printer; color sheets, complete with registration marks, will be printed. To print on a T-shirt, overlays were sent to a screen-printing vendor along with PMS color numbers. This was done using FreeHand on a Macintosh.

Sibyl Moss, "Desert Pronghorns"
Designed using Adobe Illustrator on a Macintosh.

learning curve on the road toward productivity, and provides intuitive onscreen tools or commands, it is said to have a "user-friendly interface."

On the other hand, if the program has a lot of cryptic commands or possesses its own unique but difficult-to-master tools, and if the learning curve for the program is initially steep, it may receive the polite label "expertware" from program reviewers.

Another universally important feature among software is the ability to import and export files to and from other software applications and, in many cases, among other brands of computers. Compatibility with other page layout programs, which increasingly feature their own powerful graphic manipula-

tion tools, is important to graphic designers.

NETWORKING?

If you work in an office where a network of computers exists, it's probably important to consider whether the software you choose is compatible with your computer network. Not all software is networkable, nor can any programs be shared without a site license or a specifically modified version of the program that can operate on a network. In many desktop publishing environments, connectivity and the ability to interchange files, perhaps among different brands of computers on the same network, are important considerations when choosing appropriate software.

CONSULTING A SERVICE BUREAU AND JOINING A COMPUTER USER'S GROUP

Finally, consulting with the service bureau you'll use for output of your graphics is highly recommended. Your service bureau must also carry a current copy of your software plus its own sets of your high-resolution typefaces. (See Chapter Six: How to Work With Service Bureaus.)

Consulting your local service bureau is a good way to find out about other computer artists who might work nearby. Call, visit and consult with them. Maybe there's a computer user's group you could join (or you could help organize one). This is a great way to learn about new computers and software products. At the very least, you can all share your trials and tribulations. There is something else you can share, too. User's groups are frequently eligible for software discounts and other benefits like opportunities to test and evaluate "beta" versions of new software.

MacPaint

DeskPaint

SuperPaint

SuperPaint (a more painterly look)

PixelPaint

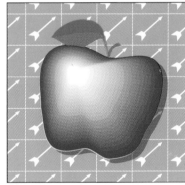
Aldus FreeHand

Gary Olsen, untitled
The look you're after will often drive your software choice. (Top left) This simple MacPaint graphic was painted small and enlarged to exaggerate the pixeled look. (Bottom left) The background of this graphic painted in PixelPaint is a simple fill pattern. (Bottom right) The background of this graphic, which was painted in Aldus FreeHand, was created using a "tiling" command that repeats a small graphic element in a neat grid pattern.

COMBINING PAINT AND DRAW PROGRAMS

DALI

This demo involves the combination of two different graphic programs in the Macintosh environment—a simple monochrome paint application (DeskPaint) as a sketching tool and a high-resolution graphics program (Aldus FreeHand) for your finished work. You could probably be happy with the results of a low-resolution paint program. But if you want to export the drawing to a document requiring a smoother look for publishing, you can always import your bit-map graphic in Free-Hand or Adobe Illustrator and "auto-trace" it, which you'll see in this demo. You will be effectively converting a bit-map to a vector

graphic that can output to a PostScript printing device (laser printer or imagesetter) with very fine lines and smooth graduated fill patterns. And you can always add color.

Auto-trace is an extremely useful tool. It can trace virtually any image you can import into the programs that feature automatic tracing. Adobe Illustrator, Aldus FreeHand and Micrografx Designer import a variety of image formats—TIFF, Paint, PICT—for just this purpose. Read your drawing program's instructions on compatible formats and how it works in your particular program.

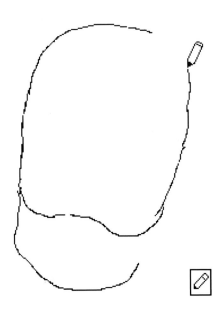

1. With the pencil tool, begin a contour drawing of the head. In this portrait, you want an upturned face framed by streaming tendrils of hair. Let's just get the face and key features established first.

YOUR PAINT PROGRAM TOOLS:

Direct rendering tools: Spray can, paint bucket, paintbrush, pencil, eraser, arc tool, and straight line tool.

Movement tools: The marquee box selects the pixeled image including the surrounding white area. The lasso selects pixels but only includes the white area surrounded by closed paths of pixels.

YOUR DRAWING TOOLS:

Freehand drawing tool and knife tool: These are among the most important tools in this lesson. The knife tool is used in Aldus FreeHand for cutting apart closed shapes. By clicking on the knife and then clicking on a vector point of a selected shape, the point will divide in two, severing the contiguous line. In Adobe Illustrator, this tool is represented by a scissors icon but functions in a similar manner.

Auto-tracing tool: It works like a marquee box, but when it surrounds an imported bit-map or graphic used as a template, it automatically plots the vectors and draws the lines. As handy as this is, the tracing is not perfect, and you will have to do some editing, line manipulation, and redrawing. The select tool (arrow) is used to select various elements you have drawn or traced for manipulation, duplication, or deletion.

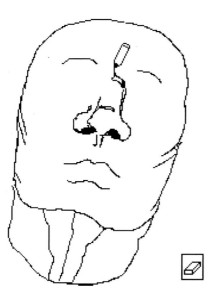

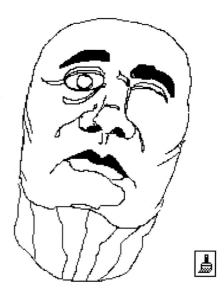

2. Contours of the face, shadows, character lines, etc., should be drawn as outlines. Besides the pencil, your most useful tool will probably be the eraser.

3. The nostrils are represented by solid black. So are the moustache, brows, upper lip and other areas of the face that represent the darkest elements of the compostion. The best tool for this is the brush tool, since it can be made into different widths and shapes.

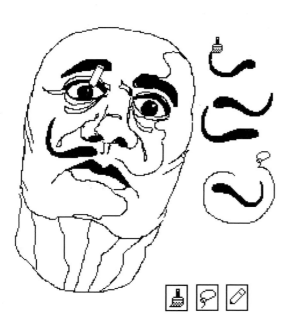

4. The moustache is more difficult to render. So you don't disturb what you have already drawn, it's best to paint the two halves of the moustache off to the side. Using the lasso tool, select the elements of the moustache and drag them to the exact place you want them. The highlights in the eye were made with the pencil. Clicking on a black pixel turns it white. The pencil, therefore, behaves like a pixel-by-pixel eraser.

5. With the pencil, complete the shapes of the hair. Don't resign yourself to a particular line or shape. Remember, you're working with a computer. You can erase and redraw to your heart's content without fear of burning a hole through your paper. This might be a good time to print your graphic to see how it actually looks on paper.

6. Oops, check this—a few broken lines need tending. Missing pixels may cause a problem with the auto-trace tool in your drawing program. Use the pencil to close up those pixel paths that defime shapes. Notice, too, that the eye lines have been changed slightly with the pencil tool.

7. That nose looks funny. Maybe the shadow lines are on the wrong side. No problem. Select the nose with the lasso tool, copy it off to the side, flip it horizontally, and use the rotation tool to recreate the precise angle.

8. Dali, rendered in my paint program. It's almost ready for transporting to Aldus FreeHand for auto-tracing. As I mentioned, a drawing with well-defined lines traces best. FreeHand's auto-trace feature prefers lines a little thicker than in the original.

9. To thicken up the lines quickly, merely surround the graphic with a marquee box. Depress your mouse key with the select arrow positioned on any one of the corners of the marquee box. Keep depressing the mouse button and then depress the shift key simultaneously while dragging the corner of the box inward. This maneuver allows you to reduce the drawing in perfect aspect ratio, but the lines stay their original thickness. Save the result in the appropriate format for importation by your drawing program.

10. We've imported the bit-map drawing of Dali into FreeHand. By selecting the auto-trace tool and encircling the graphic, the auto-trace function begins. It may take several seconds. I'm very happy with this result. I see distinct individual shapes that can be manipulated. In some cases, however, shapes have converged, like around the eyes. These shapes may have to be separated using the blade tool, which cuts apart the vector paths.

11. In manipulating the various lines in this graphic, you may discover a few that can be eliminated. You may also discover that you're spending a lot of time fiddling with various details. Rather than waste time, a good strategy is to redraw some additional shapes with the freehand tool to overlay on top of your graphic. The eyes— pupils and lids—are an example of this technique. Remember— working with a computer drawing program of this type is like sculpting with shapes of paper.

12. Each enclosed shape can now attain line and fill information. In FreeHand, there are two separate menus—one for line attributes and one for fills (patterns, shades of gray, colors, radial, linear and blended). Here, you see various shades of gray rendered in graduated and radial fills. The tendrils of hair are individual shapes with graduated fills from light gray (10 percent) to black. The shapes have no line attributes. The eyelids and pupil circles are shades of gray. The tie is an assembage of shapes with radial fills from white to 40 percent gray.

13. Here, all shapes have been given fill attributes and, as a group, have been assigned black outlines. Even the white portion of the face possesses a specified fill, which is white, and an outline, which is black. Ultimately, you want to eliminate the lines and let the individual shades of gray define the planes and details of the face.

14. The final Dali portrait—all shapes have assigned fills, but under the line menu, we have specified "none." Even though there are no lines, the object-oriented shapes can still exist.

DRAWING ON A MICROCOMPUTER

Creating art with high-resolution drawing programs.

What clearly distinguishes a drafting or PostScript drawing program from a paint program is that drawing applications are designed to run a variety of high-resolution output devices—usually intended for publishing. Paint programs are mainly bit-map graphics applications. A paint graphic's output resolution on a laser printer, for example, is only as good as its screen resolution.

Drafting and drawing programs, on the other hand, were created in a programming code (most likely Adobe PostScript), designed to drive desktop laser machines and high-resolution image processors. These processors render extremely smooth and uniform type, lines, fills, colors and blends.

HIGH-RESOLUTION PRINTING DEVICES
How do they re-create graphics with smooth lines and even tones?
The process by which graphics—72 dots per inch on your screen—become smooth 300 dpi output from

Max Seabaugh, "Learning"
Seabaugh used Adobe Illustrator on a Macintosh to create this illustration for Dow Jones Business Publications.

your laser printer is not as complex as it might seem. Laser printers just have higher resolution bit-maps than your computer monitor. Raster image processors, like the Linotronic or Compugraphic Imagesetter, can reproduce your graphic images at 1,270 dpi up to 2,540 dpi. These high-resolution devices convert vector images (like those produced by a PostScript drawing program) to raster images of a very high resolution. This image converter is called a raster image processor (RIP).

VECTORS CREATE PATHS, LINES FOLLOW PATHS
Drafting and PostScript drawing programs create object-oriented graphics, and both produce graphics of high resolution. With object-oriented graphics, lines you inscribe on your computer's screen are plotted by a series of vector points that define a path for the lines to follow. If the end of the line is brought around to join its point of origin, which closes the path, shazam! A shape is formed. You must understand how a drawing program treats lines and shapes:
1. Lines are actually paths drawn between vector points.
2. Shapes are formed when the line path encloses a space, e.g., the end of the line or series of connected lines (as in a rectangle, trapezoid,

ellipse or irregular shape) is joined to its point of origin.

In PostScript and most object-oriented drafting programs, shapes are formed with specialized shape tools or freehand tools. All shapes are defined by a series of vectors and all shapes can be modified by manipulating those vectors.
3. Fills or colors can only occupy shapes made up of closed paths or objects.
4. Objects are made up of an assemblage of lines, shapes and fills grouped together to be one (in a PostScript program). In a drafting program, objects such as a "square" are defined as such from the outset. A square can become a rectangle, but it still has two sets of parallel lines and four 90-degree angles. A circle can become an oval, but never a square.
5. Layers—each individual line, shape or object (an assemblage of lines and shapes that have been grouped to form a single object) occupies its own layer on your drawing. The more objects you add to your composition, the more layers you work with.

DRAFTING AND DRAWING VERSUS PAINTING PROGRAMS
Why choose a drawing or drafting program rather than a paint program? On microcomputers that

Karen Jacobi, untitled
Texas artist Jacobi works with Micrografx Designer, a PostScript drawing program for IBM PC-type systems.

drive laser printers or high-resolution image processors, drawing programs specialize in smoother, higher resolution line art and typefaces. Paint programs, on the other hand, give you less defined resolution of the pixelmap on which you render images. In paint programs, your output usually matches the resolution of your screen display. Traditionally, at the low end of the technology, if your screen resolution is 72 dpi, your paint program's output will be 72 dpi. In a draw program, your screen resolution is still 72 dpi, but you can get output of up to nearly 4,000 dpi (depending on your output device).

It is only when you venture into the realm of high-resolution bitmap programs, which require graphic boards powerful enough to display 16, 24 or 32 bit-per-pixel resolution, that you can deliver smooth line work and fine screen gradation. These applications work with a reduced view of an enlarged graphic. In other words, you still work at the pixel resolution of your computer's display, but your output device will address a very large image. Large images on the bitmap, when reduced, reduce the size of the pixels, too. Smaller pixels mean higher resolution.

Drawing programs, particularly PostScript drawing programs like Adobe Illustrator, Micrografx Designer, CorelDRAW and Aldus FreeHand, have powerful built-in color printing and separating tools. Since many designers use such programs in publishing applications, these programs offer a choice of color models in which you can prepare your graphic for printing—process color (with separations for four inks: cyan, magenta, yellow and black, often abbreviated as CMYK), or spot color including Pantone or Matchprint ink standard colors. Developing graphics that can specify these widely accepted color standards is important to the designer or illustrator who works on commercial assignments that utilize color.

THE EVOLUTION OF DRAWING PROGRAMS

The first generation of off-the-shelf drawing programs for microcomputers was extremely two-dimensional. They created rectangles, ellipses and polygons very well. These programs could specify line thickness and create fill patterns, but weren't nearly as sophisticated as current drawing software. Such wonders as a truly freehand drawing tool, handy auto-tracing, and several other tools found in programs such as Aldus FreeHand (Mac and IBM), Deneba's Canvas (Mac), Adobe Illustrator (Mac and IBM), CorelDRAW (IBM) and Micrografx Designer (IBM), took a lot of time and programming talent to develop and bring to the marketplace.

Now, a single drawing program, like Adobe Illustrator, can serve as an artist's or designer's primary tool. It, and a variety of other programs in its class, is used to produce anything from presentation graphics and illustrations for publishing, to designs for clothing and consumer product packaging.

"DO YOU ACTUALLY DRAW WITH THAT MOUSE?"

The process of drawing on a computer is quite different from traditional methods, at least for me. For one thing, I don't look at my hand or the surface on which it rests. For some artists, this is a difficult skill to develop, but I was challenged by it. I used to draw exclusively with the mouse and became accomplished at it. I tried other devices, such as pens and trackballs (dreadful for drawing), but none was what I was looking for. Then

along came the pressure-sensitive tablet. New versions of my favorite software, like FreeHand, began offering special onscreen tools that took advantage of the pressure-sensitive stylus. This is a powerful innovation, and much of my latest work in FreeHand (available on both the Mac and PC) reflects a wonderful spontaneity that only this stylus can provide. I personally use Wacom's stylus for ease and comfort, although there are other tablets with different features at different prices.

As you get more comfortable with the computer, you'll develop your own drawing shortcuts. For example, I've found that just because you work with a mouse-driven computer, every single stroke isn't drawn with the mouse. I've developed a two-handed method of rendering—my left hand is on the keyboard for keystroke

Sibyl Moss, "Sanibel Island"
Sweatshirt design created with Adobe Illustrator on a Macintosh.

Kathy Roling, "Cycle Shop Billboard"
(Above) Kathy works for an outdoor advertising firm. Virtually all of her designs are prepared on a Macintosh.

Kathy Roling, "KAT Billboard"
(Right) This outdoor advertisement was prepared in Aldus FreeHand. Type elements were scanned from reflective art and auto-traced, and the cat was drawn with the freehand tool. This graphic will become a billboard 14 feet high and 48 feet long.

shortcuts, and my right hand is on the mouse.

If you're a beginner, drawing on a computer can take more time than drawing with a pencil. It took many hours to prepare my first computer illustration because I was involved in the learning process.

Where you really gain in productivity, however, is in the modification and pre-press preparation of your illustration. You control your graphic like never before. Do you want to make major color changes? Redraw a large section

of the art? No problem! And with most of these programs' spot-color and color separation capabilities, you can prepare a complete press-ready piece of art in about the same time it took you to execute a comp.

MY APPROACH TO ILLUSTRATING ON COMPUTER

Thumbnails still continue to be the first step I take when constructing a drawing. Instead of drawing on a tissue, however, I render a monochromatic drawing in a simple paint program like Zedcor's

DeskPaint, a program designed for the Macintosh. For most of my illustrations, I use two of the many drawing and painting tools available in the program—the pencil (draws a one-pixel-width line) and the eraser.

First I draw a cartoonlike sketch, usually with no fills or shades. I prefer to use line-drawn shapes to show where my shading or colors will eventually be. Frequently, for shapes that must be uniform or symmetrical, I draw a contour of half of my object as if it were split down the middle. I copy it, flip it horizontally, and attach it to my first line, creating a symmetrical shape.

Once I've rendered an acceptable contour drawing, I save a copy of it in a separate file for importation to a high-resolution drawing program like Adobe Illustrator or Aldus FreeHand. I could export my drawing to other programs, including other paint programs that offer color paint palettes. However, I must first save my cartoon in a computer file format that's acceptable to the final drawing program.

After I've saved a copy, I return to my original DeskPaint drawing and play with fills and patterns. I'm then ready to print and see how the drawing looks on paper.

It's when I work with my drawing in FreeHand that I use the incredible power of the computer. At this stage, I can refine or embellish my illustration, preparing it for pre-press. I have seldom had trouble transferring a file, but others have. It seems that even if you save a drawing in the proper format for export, you may still sometimes find the appearance and resolution of the image have changed slightly when opened in another program. Fonts may be changed also. Differences in the way applications store and import files coupled with possible file format irregularities may cause this. You may be able

to correct it in the new program or try to save and import again.

TOO MANY CHOICES OR POSSIBILITIES CAN BE OVERWHELMING

When creating art on a computer, you deal with a precise, mathematical instrument that displays a line only after it has calculated the line's coordinates on the screen. It happens automatically and quickly, but it's important to remember that every line, every shape, every object on the screen is there because the computer calculates the mathematical code in your program's background to render them. Fortunately, computer program designers have created a user-friendly environment that protects us from thinking about all of this.

In most good drawing programs, we are reasonably free to just create.

Michael Gilmore, "Video Freak"
Gilmore prepared this illustration for the *Sun News*, Myrtle Beach, South Carolina, using FreeHand on a Macintosh.

Unfortunately for some of us, the computer's vast power sometimes gives us too many choices, impinging on our spontaneity. Line path, line thickness, degree of angle, curve, ellipse, fill pattern, color and placement of drawing layers can all be controlled. These are factors you must consider with a computer, when previously, you just reached for the right pencil. Being faced with the list of choices is like being locked in the art supply store after closing. For some artists, this responsibility and power is, at first, overwhelming.

WORKING IN LAYERS

Let's say you've completed a composition made up of several overlapping objects and lines. Imagine your drawing as a pile of perfectly clear Mylar sheets with each element you introduce occupying its own layer.

Now you want to change an underlying shape. Navigate below the more recently drawn objects and layers you've created to get to your target object, which is likely on the bottom layer.

Fortunately, tools are available in your program to help you manipulate objects and layers so at the click of a button you can bring an underlying shape to the top, modify it, and return it to any layer you wish.

Gary Olsen, "Bones"
(Above) A textile design prepared in Adobe Illustrator.

John F. Sherman, "Unconventional Notation"
(Right) Sherman is Professor of Design at Notre Dame University. He uses computers that generate PostScript object-oriented graphics, which he outputs to an Allied Linotronic.

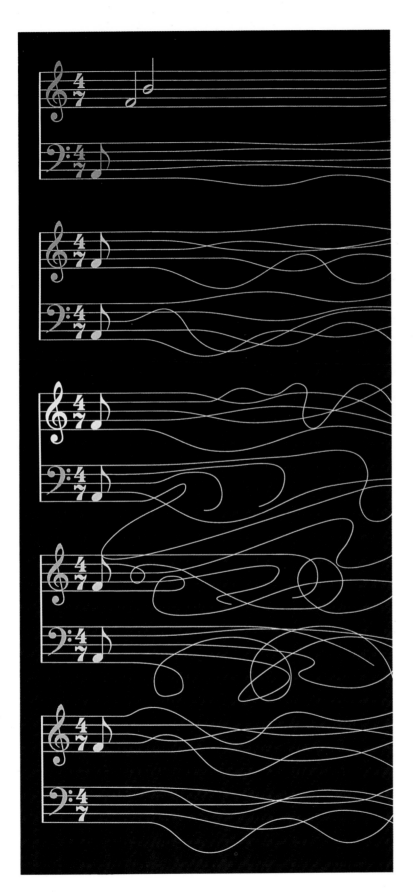

BRING TO FRONT, SEND TO BACK, PASTE IN BACK, PASTE IN FRONT (WHEW!)

A problem with drawing in layers is that lines and objects that become trapped below other, more recently drawn items, are sometimes hard to locate and move if you need to modify them. Bring to Front, Send to Back, Paste in Back, and Paste in Front are some of the more common elemental commands used by object-oriented drawing programs for shuffling layers.

Consult your individual software instructions to learn exactly how these tools work. In the better programs, you have full layer control of objects. In the program I use the most, Aldus FreeHand, I have 200 definable layers, which allow me to underdraw or overdraw without disturbing what I've already drawn. Multiply these layers times the number of naturally occurring layers formed with each new element you draw in your composition. If you were using traditional tools, you would have a stack of tissue vellums 4 feet high!

GROUPING AND JOINING LINES, SHAPES AND OBJECTS

Now that you understand the layer concept, we'll discuss how you can combine objects from two different layers to form one easy-to-manipulate object on one layer.

Commands such as Group or Join Elements keep your drawing from becoming an unwieldy collection of small and separate elements that can make modification almost impossible. Imagine wanting to change the thickness of one line located below 50 separately rendered objects.

The potential difficulties that layering poses makes it a good idea to group together small objects from time to time to economize on layering. Anything grouped or joined can be ungrouped and unjoined if you have to modify an individual

Sibyl Moss, "Coyotes"
Colorado artist Sibyl Moss specializes in graphics for clothing. Her illustrated T-shirts are created with Adobe Illustrator, which produces excellent spot-color separations for screen-printing.

element again. Practice how to strategize, and you will quickly develop some of your own techniques in object and layer management.

THE TECHNIQUE OF LAYERING SHAPES

In the demonstration portions of this book, I've emphasized and attempted to capitalize on the idiosyncrasies of the most typical drawing programs. Most object-oriented drawing programs operate with the same, or at least very similar, tools; regardless of the differences in tools and commands, the results are usually the same—the creation of a vector-based graphic element.

My drawings are made up of shapes layered on top of one another. I liken the process to paper sculpting—cutting out individual pieces of paper and pasting them on top of one another to build an illusion of depth. I enhance the illusion by using graduated fills and radial fills to bring specific areas of my drawing closer to or farther away from the viewer. My illustration of Salvador Dali, pages 54-59 is a good example of my drawing strategy. Each element of his portrait is a shape defined by a closed path. The fills are a combination of graduated (the tendrils of hair) or radial fills (the tie and some of the shadow portions of the face). Even the thick and thin lines, which appear to have been rendered by a broad nibbed pen or brush, are actually shapes.

DRAWING TOOLS

Rendering tools for drawing, tracing and line work.

• **A line tool** enables you to draw straight lines. Menu options allow you to change the thickness, pattern

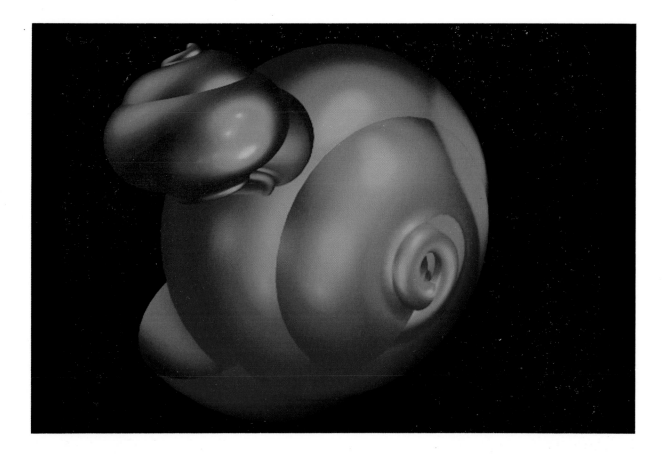

James Dowlen, "Spiral 4A"
Created using Time Arts Lumina on an Everex computer.

or color of the line.

• **A freehand drawing tool** enables you to draw curvy lines and shapes.

• **A Bézier curve tool** allows you to draw precise curves with greater control than a freehand drawing tool allows.

SHAPE TOOLS

Menu choices enable you to fill these shapes with a solid color, pattern or shade of gray.

• **A circle tool** makes circles or ellipses (some programs feature a separate ellipse tool).

• **A rectangle tool** makes squares or rectangles.

• **A "coupon" or rounded corner rectangle tool** allows you to make rectangles with perfectly rounded corners. Menu options, available in most programs, enable you to change the radius of the rounded corners.

• **A polygon tool** allows you to make multisided shapes composed of straight lines. Click at various points, and a series of straight lines will follow you. Return and click on your point of origin and your shape will be complete.

In advanced drawing programs, you may have the following:

• **A skew tool**, which enables you to skew or distort at an angle your graphic element or a copy of it (like italicizing type).

• **A reflect tool**, which creates a mirror image or a mirrored copy of your graphic element. It can flip it vertically, horizontally or at an angle.

• **A spin tool (also called a free-rotation tool)** that enables you to rotate your graphic element around an anchor point at any angle you choose.

• **Auto-trace**, which allows you to import a graphic from another source or a scanned image. It may be "phantomed in" on its own draw-

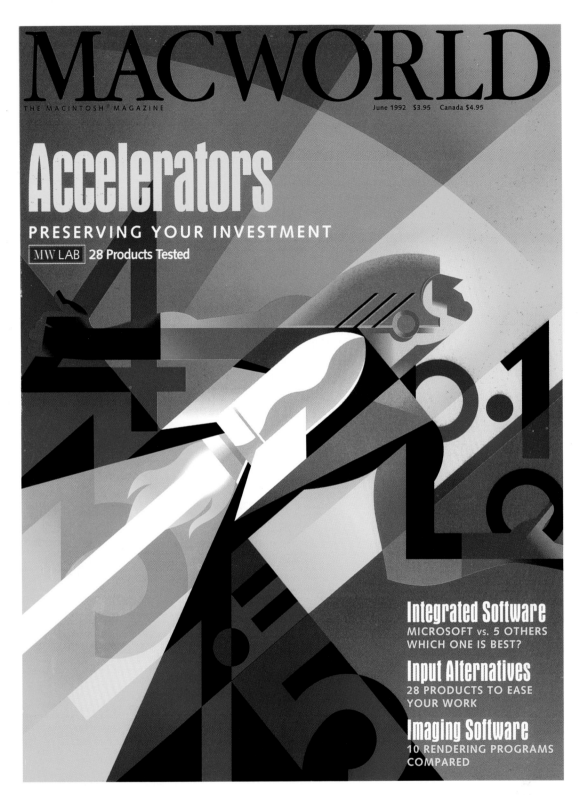

Ron Chan, "Rocket Man"
This cover for *MacWorld* magazine was made using Adobe Illustrator. Chan is one of the most successful and prolific computer artists in the United States. His work is seen regularly in the *San Francisco Chronicle* and it purposely effects the art deco look of the 1920s and 1930s. Because object-oriented programs can mimic the subtle color gradations and blends of an airbrush, graphic styles such as Early Modern, Modern, and Art Deco are experiencing a revival.

ing layer as a template. You can trace it by hand, or your computer program can trace it automatically using the *auto-trace* command.

In various microcomputer drawing programs that use PostScript, you can easily auto-trace a clean, high-contrast graphic. However, with a poor reference image—one lacking sharp detail or contrast—the auto-traced results can be a jumbled mess. In many cases, you might waste time cleaning up an auto-traced image that might have been easier to draw yourself. This feature is constantly being improved, however.

DEFINING PATHS WITH CORNER AND CURVE POINTS

A series of vector points connected by a line forms a path. There are open paths (lines) and closed paths (lines that form shapes).

In Adobe Illustrator, Aldus FreeHand and Micrografx Designer, there is a basic similarity in how vector points are defined. All have freehand drawing tools that allow you to draw a line or shape with all vertices displayed when you're finished drawing. These programs also feature curve points and corner points. But in Illustrator, any vector point (called anchor points in this program) can be a corner point or a curve point, depending on how you position the point "handles" or direction lines. Yes, it sounds confusing. The lines that emanate from these points are either curved or straight, depending on how you position these direction lines.

PREVIEW AND DRAWING SCREENS

The "preview" features of Illustrator, FreeHand and Micrografx all vary, and it's a matter of personal preference as to which program is easiest to use. In Illustrator, you must draw in one screen (which shows the even weight PostScript path), but you must "preview" your illus-

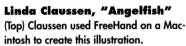

Linda Claussen, "Angelfish"
(Top) Claussen used FreeHand on a Macintosh to create this illustration.

Gary Olsen, "Seabirds"
(Bottom) Object-oriented drawing programs are precise in rendering lines. To make my line work appear hand-rendered, I positioned smaller white shapes atop larger black ones. At right is the line work minus color fills.

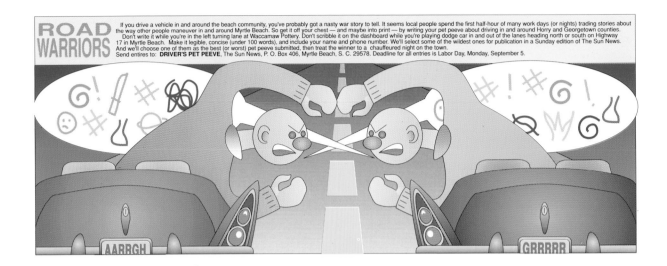

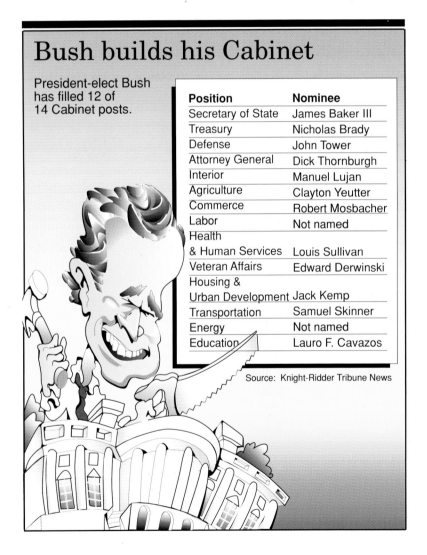

Bush builds his Cabinet

President-elect Bush has filled 12 of 14 Cabinet posts.

Position	Nominee
Secretary of State	James Baker III
Treasury	Nicholas Brady
Defense	John Tower
Attorney General	Dick Thornburgh
Interior	Manuel Lujan
Agriculture	Clayton Yeutter
Commerce	Robert Mosbacher
Labor	Not named
Health & Human Services	Louis Sullivan
Veteran Affairs	Edward Derwinski
Housing & Urban Development	Jack Kemp
Transportation	Samuel Skinner
Energy	Not named
Education	Lauro F. Cavazos

Source: Knight-Ridder Tribune News

Michael Gilmore, "Road Warriors"
(Above) Using FreeHand on a Macintosh, Gilmore created this illustration for the *Sun News*, Myrtle Beach, South Carolina.

Jeff Goertzen, "George Bush"
(Left) Since the computer is such a flexible illustration tool offering myriad possibilities, it's hard to know when an illustration is actually finished.

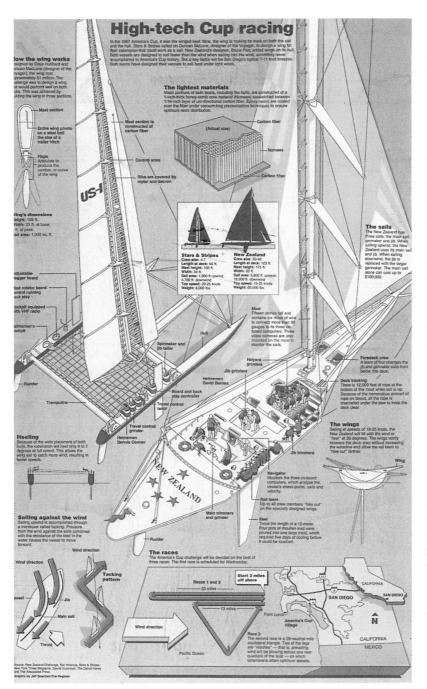

tration in a nondrawable window to see what it actually looks like. On a large monitor, you can open both the draw screen and the preview screen, drawing in one window as the image changes in the other.

In the Macintosh environment, I prefer FreeHand because it allows me to draw in the preview mode. This makes it easier to see and interact with the image, but Freehand gets slower when you work in preview. When in a PostScript line mode, FreeHand runs faster and the screen refreshes a bit faster. With complex illustrations, this can be an important consideration. On the IBM, Micrografx Designer offers features identical to both Illustrator and FreeHand, but like FreeHand, Designer lets you draw in the preview mode.

HOW TO APPROACH THESE DRAWING DEMONSTRATIONS

My advice is to develop some familiarity with your computer's software before you tackle these lessons. The software changes so rapidly, offering more features with every incarnation, that it would have been futile to write a keystroke-by-keystroke manual. Just do your best to copy the evolving pictures. Don't feel compelled to duplicate exactly what you see on these pages; just go with your creative flow.

Jeff Goertzen, "New Zealand"
Goertzen is a newspaper illustrator who uses Aldus FreeHand and a Macintosh to draw graphics for the *Orange County Register*, Orange County, California.

We begin this lesson with a very simple bit-map rendering of a rose prepared in a monochrome paint program. Our objective is to import the sketch in a PostScript drawing program like Aldus FreeHand (Mac), Adobe Illustrator (Mac and IBM PC) or Micrografx Designer (IBM PC). These advanced drawing programs feature auto-tracing.

You never know just how complete the auto-trace will be. More often than not, you must clip the vector paths to separate shapes and redraw some elements (for a more complete discussion of auto-tracing, see the Dali demonstration). If your approach to graphic design calls for a lot of tracing, consider a dedicated tracing program that turns a variety of bit-map images into PostScript line art. The first of its kind is Adobe's Streamline, a programmable auto-trace tool that features high-speed performance.

Take a look at Step Two in this demonstration. This is a screen snapshot of a freshly auto-traced bit-map. The resulting shapes that were traced have been selected to reveal their grabbers or handlers, which, when moved individually, change the path of the line. This particular program is Aldus FreeHand—it's similar to Illustrator and Designer. With Free-Hand, you can draw lines with a freehand tool and the vectors are automatically plotted along the path you've created. Or you can click vector points on your screen and a line follows them.

I often describe drawing in a PostScript graphic program as "paper sculpting." Think of your graphic in terms of an assemblage of overlapping shapes. Each of these shapes possesses line and fill characteristics you specify from menus of choices. A graphic is the result of a building process that requires a well-planned strategy. With practice, you will develop your own stylistic approach and shortcuts.

Pictured on the right are two different toolboxes, but they have similar tools. The short box is from Aldus FreeHand. You can position it anywhere on the screen that's comfortable. The tall box is from Adobe Illustrator and resides on the left margin of the screen. I pulled out the tools from both boxes that function almost the same but are represented onscreen by different icons. The top icons are the reflect or mirror image tools. The second pair represents the auto-trace tools (in Free-Hand, you surround the object being traced; in Illustrator, you touch every edge of the object you want traced). The third pair of icons represents the tool that cuts or clips paths and shapes. The bottom pair of tools are for slanting objects.

FreeHand Toolbox

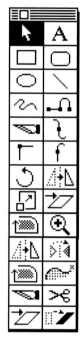

Illustrator Toolbox

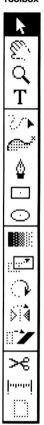

POSTSCRIPT DRAWING TOOLS USED IN THIS LESSON:

Auto-tracing and shape editing tools: Once the bit-map image has been imported, you can use the auto-trace tool to encircle the object. The program will automatically plot PostScript vectors and lines. You will probably want to separate some of the resulting shapes, so you'll use the knife tool. Activate the knife tool, click on a vector point, and the vector divides into two separate points and opens the shape.

Freehand drawing tool: This will be your most useful tool. Draw your line or shape, and the vector points are automatically plotted.

Shape manipulation tools: The reflection (or mirror image) tool, the free rotation tool, and the stretch tool allow you to manipulate and change shapes or groups of shapes.

1. We begin with the importation of a template—in this case, a bit-map rendering of wild roses. The lines are well defined, which will make for a promising auto-trace. To activate the auto-trace in this particular PostScript drawing program, merely select the appropriate icon from the toolbox and surround the item you want traced.

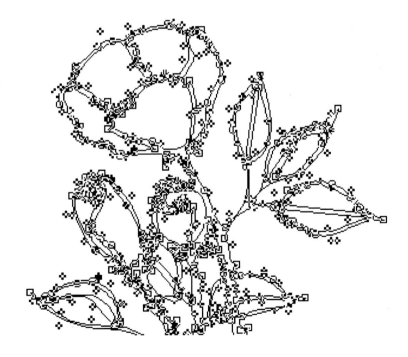

2. If your original graphic is complex, the auto-tracing can take a long time, perhaps several minutes. This is because the computer assumes you want everything traced precisely. Negative as well as positive shapes in your original are traced and turned into vector-defined shapes. All of the vector points and point handles are revealed in this tracing.

3. Auto-tracing is somewhat imprecise, and no doubt you'll have to cut and separate some of the resulting contiguous shapes. By selecting the knife tool and clicking on various vector points, the lines and shapes can be separated or rejoined with other points, and some points can be eliminated to cut down on the number of vectors you must deal with. In many cases, it's too time-consuming to perform this kind of surgery. Often I draw new shapes to lay atop something, much like constructing a paper sculpture. Note the freehanded bud leaf drawn off to the side. It can be selected and moved into place.

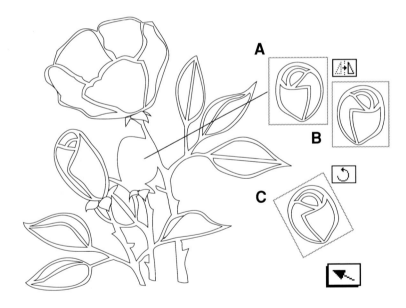

4. The middle rosebud appeared to be drawn backward in the original. Now is the time to change it. The petals should overlap the buds from right to left. The center bud overlaps left to right. By using the select tool (arrow) and selecting the components of the bud as a group, they can be moved to the side. (On the Mac, hold the shift key while selecting the various shapes.) The steps required to flop the bud are as follows: **A.** With the select tool, draw a marquee box around the rosebud shape. From the Element menu in FreeHand, select the Group command. This will make the bud a single unit; **B.** Select the reflect tool and click on the bud. The image will turn into a mirror image of itself, but it will be tilting the wrong direction; **C.** Choose the rotation tool and click on the bud. By holding the mouse button down and moving the mouse, you'll be able to tilt the bud at precisely the right angle. With the select tool, move the bud back into the graphic. Ungroup it so you can color the individual elements later.

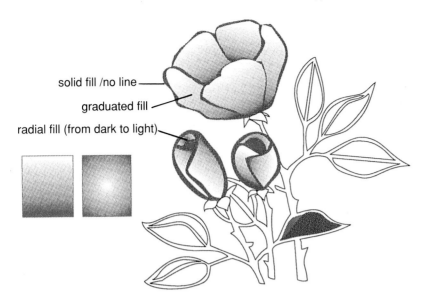

solid fill /no line

graduated fill

radial fill (from dark to light)

5. Keep two things in mind when working with PostScript drawing programs: line and fill. This is a good time to decide what kind of line you want for this graphic: How thin or thick? What color? Your program's line menu gives you infinite choices. Fills can be a solid color, a graduated shade or a radial shade. The two squares at the far left represent graduated and radial shading. The green leaf is composed of two shapes, each filled with its own solid hue of green. No line has been specified on the components of the leaf. The stem and outline of the leaves will be facilitated by a complex shape filled with a third, darker hue of green.

6. At virtually any stage of your drawing, you have endless opportunities to experiment. For example, if the shading in the illustration above looks a little flat, you could overlay some freehanded elements at the base of the blossom and fill them with a darker hue. When you start overlapping shapes, you may have to use the Bring to Front and Send to Back commands. You are working in layers, and occasionally those layers become shuffled. Some of the overlaying elements have been rendered off to the side. The unfilled outlines at the far right show precisely what was drawn for two of the blossom's elements.

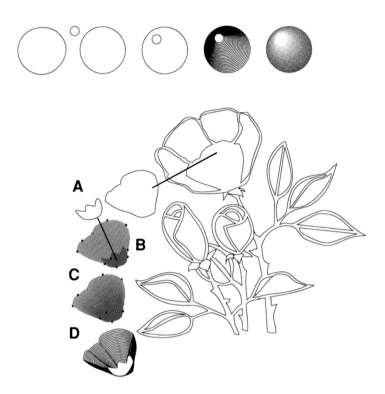

Blending shapes in a PostScript drawing program is a simple process. The sphere effect is an excellent illustration of how blending works. The large circle is the sphere, the small circle represents the highlight—two distinct shapes. The small circle is placed in the large circle and assigned a dark fill. The Blend command is activated to blend the two circles together. The program creates the blend by drawing a series of intermittent circles. To create a smooth transition of color, specify no line attributes to your original circles. The black line rendering is the PostScript line version of the smoothly colored sphere to its right.

1. A PostScript drawing program's specialty is blending shapes. For example, remove one of the petal shapes from your original line drawing. **A.** With the freehand tool, draw a small shape similar to the one at right. **B.** Assign a dark red fill to it, specify no line, and overlay the shape at the base of the large petal. **C.** Select two points from each shape and activate the Blend command in the Elements menu. Select at least twenty blending steps. **D.** This is the PostScript line model of the petal blend.

2. Continue your strategy with each of the petal shapes, drawing a small shape and nesting it inside of the larger. Assign a dark hue to the smaller shape and light hue to the larger shape. Selecting like points on both shapes, execute the Blend command from the Elements menu and specify at least twenty steps. At left, I have superimposed the PostScript line model of the top petal to illustrate what is taking place. Your main tools at this stage are your Select tool and FreeHand Drawing tool.

3. For the most part, you can delete the old leaf shapes and draw some new, simpler ones to facilitate your blends. The new leaves should be completely separate elements from the stems. For the upturned leaf, a blended shape can be overlaid with a solid dark-green shape that represents the upturned bottom portion of the leaf toward the viewer. You can add some interesting highlight shapes to the blossom; the shapes, shown off to the side, have been assigned graduated fills from light pink to red.

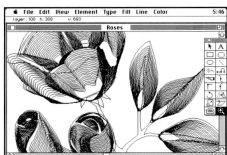

4. A simple flower it isn't. The PostScript line view in the screen snapshot above dramatically illustrates how a computer interprets rounded shapes as a series of closely spaced polygons. Drawing this rose probably took you a good deal more time than if you had used traditional tools, and that's typical in the beginning. Though you sometimes spend more time in executing some pieces of computer art, you will spend less time changing, modifying, or integrating your illustration into a total design solution.

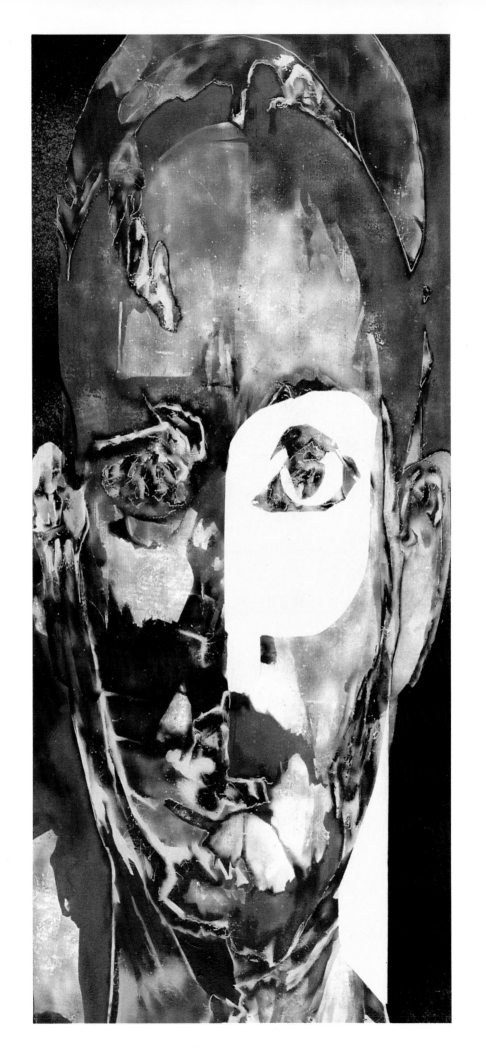

PAINTING ON A COMPUTER

Creating art with computer paint programs.

The great thing about creating art on the computer is the capability to make changes quickly and easily. You can fiddle with your art without ever running the risk of a piece being overworked.

Nowhere is this more beguiling than in the realm of computer paint programs. There is nothing like a vast and complex bit-map to play with! The bit-map is what characterizes raster paint programs from vector-based, object-oriented drawing programs. Instead of plotting your line, creating a path, and defining your shape by manipulating a series of vertices, you work with pixels. On a large display monitor (15-by-19-inch) you could be working with nearly two million of them!

PAINTING PROGRAMS
Why some are more complex and have more features than drawing programs.
Every new version of microcomputer paint programs includes more features—endless lists of key com-

. . . .

Jeremy Gardiner, untitled
Gardiner, a professor of computer graphics at New York's Pratt Institute, uses his computer as a sketch pad to create compositions. These compositions eventually find their way to canvas where he paints them with acrylics.

binations, mouse clicks, multileveled menus and special effects. It's possible to discover something new about your favorite painting program even if you've been using it every day for the past six months. By comparison, the most sophisticated PostScript drawing program is simple.

Painting programs, particularly those designed to work on color computers, are more complex than drafting or PostScript drawing programs. But once you get involved with painting programs, you'll find that they're extremely productive tools, giving you flexibility in getting your ideas down. Painting on a computer is, for the most part, a more spontaneous endeavor than drafting.

PAINTING VERSUS DRAWING OR DRAFTING
Computer draftings and PostScript drawings are easily modified because art is made up of overlapping objects rendered by your program's mathematical code. These objects can be selected and modified individually. But a computer painting is a map of pixels locked into a grid. Unlike the drawing, which is made up of many levels, a painting bit-map is one layer.

PAINTING TOOLS
A distinct advantage of painting on a computer is that you have many tools at your fingertips. Besides the usual line, geometric shape and text tools found in drawing programs, you have these basics (shown on page 83) found in most microcomputer painting programs:
- **Spray Cans and Airbrushes**—Your screen tool becomes a nozzle on a paint sprayer, and it behaves like the real thing.
- **Paintbrushes (of several sizes and shapes)**—Thin, thick, round, square and angled.
- **Paint Bucket**—Rapidly fills closed shapes.
- **Lasso and Marquee Tools**—Allow you to select specific areas of pixels and move, duplicate or cut them out of your illustration. The lasso selects just the black or colored pixels and leaves the white or uncolored ones. The marquee is similar to the lasso tool, but it selects any rectangular area of the screen and all the pixels within the area of the marquee. A lassoed image, if it isn't an enclosed shape, is transparent, whereas an area that was selected by the marquee tool is opaque.
- **Eraser**—Lets you erase mistakes and also paint in reverse. In initial rendering, the eraser is used almost as much as any other tool.

SPECIAL EFFECTS TOOLS

What follows is a list of basic image manipulation tools, essential in most microcomputer painting programs:

• **Flip Horizontally or Vertically**— Select an element of your illustration—a line, shape, piece of type or text—and command the computer to flip it horizontally or vertically 180 degrees. This is one of the most handy tools for rapid rendering of symmetrical shapes. Merely draw a half or profile of your intended shape, copy it, flip it and join the two (now opposite) halves together to form your total shape.

• **Free Rotate**—Allows you to spin an element of your illustration and position it at any angle.

• **Pencil**—Lets you draw a freehand line of one pixel width. On basic monochrome applications, you can turn individual pixels on and off on your bit-map.

• **Pen or Line Tool**—Creates a line of any pixel width, depending on the width of the line you choose among the options provided. You may also draw dotted, dashed, double, triple, thick, thin and even-patterned lines. In a full-color program, you can draw a line in any color available to you from your system.

• **Rectangle, Round Rectangle, Polygon, Ellipse Tools**—Allow you to rapidly draw these common shapes.

• **Airbrush Special Effects**—In the simpler monochrome paint programs, the spray can is a random pixel switcher. However, in high-resolution applications with 16, 24 and 32 bit-per-pixel graphics boards, you'll have the ultimate airbrush that selectively illuminates your screen's tiny phosphors within the pixels. This allows you to spray a fine line of color. You can also adjust the spray to create a coarse spatter pattern.

• **Brush Special Effects**—Brushes can do more than just give you different diameters within which to paint. You can brush on patterns from your

Tomoya Ikeda, "Oriental Goddess"
(Above) This Japanese artist uses Pixel-Paint and Studio 8 software to create detailed paint images that take up the entire screen area on a 19-inch monitor.

Tomoya Ikeda, "The Golden Dragon"
(Far left) This was created using Pixel-Paint on a Macintosh.

TYPICAL TOOLS FOUND IN A PAINT PROGRAM

Spray Can and Airbrush, Paintbrush and Paint Bucket.

Lasso and Marquee tools.

Eraser and Pencil tools.

Rectangle, Round Rectangle, Polygon and Ellipse tools.

© 1989 Charlie Athanas

Charles Athanas, "Kerosene Ran"

"Kerosene Ran" is a character created by this Chicago artist for an illustrated story called "Burning City." Athanas does a variety of computer-based illustrations for everything from comic books to animation for music videos. He used Full-Paint on a Macintosh Plus.

pattern menu and, on even the most basic paint programs, your brush can take on a variety of shapes—chisel, angle chisel, round or square. (You may even be able to program your own specialized brush shape.)

UNIQUE SPECIAL EFFECTS

The microcomputer market is awash with paint programs, each touting its most unique and indispensable feature. Here are just a few you might have available:

• **Pixelation**—Gives you the ability to specify the size of the pixel. You can make them any size larger than the minimum size in the program. So if you're after a "digital esthetic" or a big pixel look, this feature is one to watch for. Photon Paint for

the Macintosh is one program with this feature.

• **Wrapping or Encrusting**—This is becoming a popular feature among microcomputer-based paint programs. It's been a staple of high-powered computer graphics programs featuring video capture boards. Need a special texture for your subject? Capture the texture on video, cut and paste the texture into your composition, wrap it around your shape, and so on. Encrusting is taking an image captured on video or scanned into your computer, and encrusting it with another image or wrapping it around an object.

• **Stencil**—The ability to lock together all the areas of your bit-map illus-

tration where one particular color appears. This is also called color masking. This, in effect, creates a stencil much like an airbrush frisket.

• **Distort, Twist**—Does to your image just what the names imply. In paint programs that feature three-dimension or animation, these features can result in some startling effects.

• **Tiling or Pattern Making**—A simple tiling effect may include a pattern that you've created or an image you wish to repeat on a grid plane. After you've created one tile, you can repeat it in columns and rows.

• **Draping**—This special effect is found in paint programs designed for the fashion or fabric designer. The feature allows you to take a repetitive design or pattern and create a draped effect complete with folds, creases or pleats.

DEVELOPING A STRATEGY

When I began computer painting, I worked in black and white because that was all my first computer (a Macintosh Plus) could produce. I'm glad for that. Just as a traditional artist learns to do a composition in pencil before the paint tubes are uncapped, you should also approach your first computer painting monochromatically. Jumping right into the paint pot is tempting, but you may waste a lot of valuable time by not doing some quick thumbnail sketches.

A good approach is to switch from your screen colors to gray scale using your monitor's controls. You'll discover that if a computer painting doesn't work in monochrome or gray scale, it usually doesn't improve when color is added.

Gary Olsen, "Black Mountains Nocturnal"
The meteor was an afterthought — a single Bézier curve of white pixels. This was created using PixelPaint on a Macintosh.

Peter McCormick, "Sunset #1"
Created with Painter for Windows on a PC.

The beauty of working on your design in monochrome first is that you can maintain a master document of your original work and color copies of it. Then you can experiment with color variations on copies of your graphic element to determine the most effective treatment.

Another advantage to working in monochrome first is you learn to use color economically. Your work is less likely to look like a grenade went off in your paint box.

Working With Color

Understanding how the eye blends small dots of colors can work to your advantage as a computer artist. Just as Impressionist painter Georges Seurat used pointillism in masterpieces such as *A Sunday Afternoon on the Island of La Grande Jatte*, you can take advantage of the color effects created by the computer to produce some interesting pieces of art.

When Seurat painted, he knew that carefully spaced dots of bright color would be blended by the human eye some distance from the painting's surface. As the eye moves farther back from his paintings, it sees totally different colors and small bits of bright color blending to create more subtle hues.

Four-color lithographic reproduction embraces the same visual principles. Closely spaced dots of the three primary colors, combined with black and white dots, blend to create virtually every color imaginable. If you want to create a more subtle blending of hues, like those found in a pastel or watercolor, it will require a little more practice with your particular program.

Color Special Effects

• **Charcoal (or pastel)**—Allows the painter to shade transparent color

© 1986 Jim Pollock 86.8.2.10

Michael Gilmore, "Nuclear Nightmare"
(Above) Gilmore used Studio 8 on a Macintosh for this illustration.

Jim Pollock, "Indian Motif"
(Left) A Western motif prepared by using MacPaint on a Macintosh.

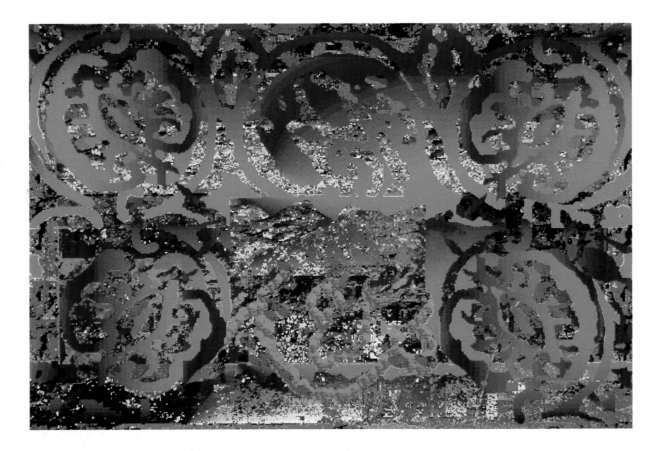

Cynthia Beth Rubin, "Marseille Carpet"
This Connecticut artist's tools were Studio 8 software — a powerful and flexible painting program — and a Macintosh.

gradually over white or another color, behaving just like a pastel.
• **Wet Paint**—An increasingly popular special effect that allows your freshly painted section to remain "wet" and movable (much like an object in a draw program), but eventually you must commit the wet paint to your illustration. (I guess that would be the "dry paint" command.)
• **Paint Over or Under (my term)**—Some programs allow you to paint a new color over something you've already painted, thereby changing the old color to the new. And it may only repaint those pixels previously painted.

Let's say you bring a scanned image into a paint program. You can overpaint the black pixels with a new color without overpainting the white background. What I call a "Paint Under" feature would allow you to paint a color under your drawing without disturbing it. Check

your software manual to see how your program refers to these features if they are available.
• **Wash, Shade or Stain**—Just as an artist uses a "glazing" technique to wash over a color and change the underlying color's hue, some paint programs can imitate this action with a *wash, shade* or *stain* command. It refers to the application of thin, transparent shades of color.
• **Color Cycling**—A rainbow or spectral effect with specific colors you select or an entire palette. Color cycling or changing colors gives the effect of movement.
• **Smear Tool**—Some color paint programs and bit-map photo retouching programs have the finger smudge tool. This allows the artist to push and smudge painted areas on the screen, softening edges, creating a rubbed-out pastel effect or an impasto oil painting effect.
• **Brushes**—Some of the new features of the current generation of

paint programs include pressure-sensitive tools. You can create brushes, for example, that have bristly hair (for dry-brush application of color) or smooth hair for even application of color.

• **Painting Tools and Effects**—Another exciting feature of some of today's paint programs is how color is applied. With Painter, for example, you can apply paint with the characteristics of transparent watercolor (complete with uneven coverage), oil paint, felt-tip color (repetitive coverage darkens the color just like a felt-tip would), pastel, colored pencil, charcoal, etc. Aldus Gallery Effects also helps you create a variety of painting effects.

• **Surfaces**—When you're finished you can emboss your work with a surface texture, make it glossy or flat, and choose the best angle of illumination. Fractal Design Painter, which offers several grades of watercolor board, canvas, weaves, rough and smooth finishes—a total of 22 surfaces—is the stand-out in terms of features here. However, Aldus Gallery Effects lets you simulate the surface of a mosaic, craquelure or fresco and do embossing.

As I began to suggest in the preceding paragraphs, Fractal Design Painter is the best example of the latest generation of computer rendering software. It mimics the tools and rendering effects of traditional art media, allowing you to select surface textures and to program brush shapes, brush behavior, color palette and media. Since I still paint on an easel as well as on a computer

Sharon Steuer, "Portrait of Jeff"
Connecticut artist Steuer used PixelPaint on a Macintosh to create this illustration.

Don Woo, "Squeeze Play"
This is an editorial illustration for an article describing current video compression routines in *Audio Visual Presentation Magazine*. Don used Studio 32 and a WACOM tablet on a Mac IIfx.

screen, trust me when I tell you that editing an oil painting on my computer is far easier and more fun than a bale of turpentine-soaked rags on my studio floor.

COMBINING GRAPHIC ELEMENTS FROM OTHER PROGRAMS

Few programs can do everything you want. Some have special effects you wish you had in others. In some computer platforms like the Macintosh, which has the same user interface from program to program, you may be able to cut and paste graphic elements from one program and transport them to another via the clipboard or scrapbook. No matter what computer program you work with, check your program's import or export features—find out if you should format your graphic element as a MacPaint file, TIFF (Tag Image File Format), EPS (Encapsulated PostScript), PICT or RIFF (Rasterized Image File Format). For example, a type manipulation effect might exist in a PostScript drawing program. Perhaps it's binding type to a curve or circle. If you export your type element to a paint program, you may lose the high resolution of the vector-based program, and the type will take on the lower resolution of your paint application.

If high-resolution type is important to your finished design, export your type to a page layout program that supports PostScript. Then import your bit-map illustration from your paint application. The success of this strategy depends on your design, but it's one way you can combine the best of both painting and drawing in one illustration.

Gary Olsen, "Linda in the Corn"
With the exception of the scanned sketch at left, this painting was prepared on a Macintosh using Fractal Design Painter software. I also employed a Wacom pressure-sensitive tablet. The artist can use a large variety of pressure-sensitive tools in Painter: pens, brushes, airbrushes, pastels, pencils, crayons, charcoals, even permanent-ink markers. Furthermore, this software provides the artist with a selection of surfaces on which to work and paint that behaves just like transparent watercolor as well as opaque oil. This collaboration of traditional art and technology is further advanced by post-production tools that increase surface texture and adjust color, brightness and contrast.

DEMO

USING COLOR PAINT PROGRAMS

THE CAROUSEL HORSE

This painting uses the color blend features included in most color paint programs. This particular subject was rendered in SuperMac's PixelPaint for the Macintosh. It uses a custom palette that includes 256 colors and various brushes, a spray can/airbrush, a smudge tool (a variation on the brush tool that pushes paint about like a wet blob of color on the end of your finger—great for blending), and a variety of fill effects—horizontal, vertical, sunburst (*radial*), and directional color blends and fades. This carousel horse was designed to take full advantage of PixelPaint's drawing and painting tools and fill effects.

My first experiences with computer paint programs were frustrat-ing. But once I learned how to use the line, curve and shape (ellipse, rectangle, trapezoid) drawing tools, I found I could draw much more rapidly. Trying to draw a smooth curve with the pencil tool is difficult even for the steadiest hand. And trying to create smooth color blends or a graduated fill with tools such as the spray can is imprecise.

The current generation of computer paint programs is almost as functional as most of the drawing programs because they treat painted elements almost like object-oriented graphics. That is where the similarity ends, however, since the high-resolution quality of PostScript drawing programs, for example, is not possible to achieve with a paint program.

TYPICAL TOOLS FOUND IN A PAINT PROGRAM:

Direct rendering tools: Spray can, paint bucket, paintbrush, pencil, eraser, arc tool, and straight line tool.

Movement tools: The marquee box selects the pixeled image including surrounding white area. The lasso selects pixels but only includes the white area surrounded by closed paths of pixels.

Shape drawing tools: Rectangle, ellipse, trapezoid, freehand shape, and rounded rectangle. Click on shaded side and the shape fills as you draw it. Click clear side, and draw an empty shape.

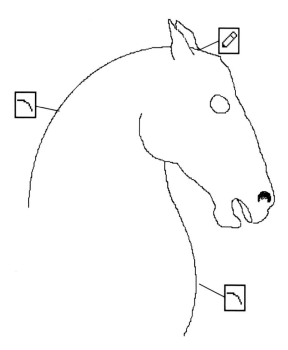

1. Initial line work is drawn with the pencil tool in black. Most of the important details will be rendered in a cartoonlike contour drawing. For long, sweeping curves, like the back of the horse's head and neck, the arc tool is an excellent way of rendering a fast, accurate line.

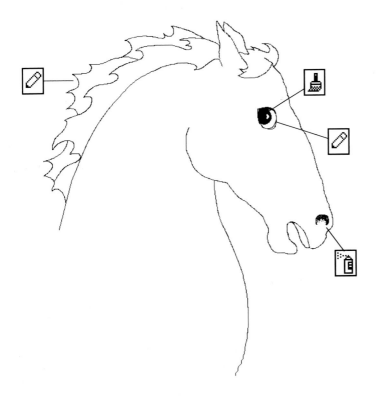

2. For solid black areas like the horse's eye, where the pencil would be too tedious, the paint brush is best. However, for the nostril, a shot from the spray can and the removal of a few pixels to form the nasal indent works well.

3. The pencil tool is still your most useful device in rendering at this stage. However, for the bridle hardware, use the circle tool. One circle inside another makes a ring.

4. Other line work is accomplished with the arc tool and the straight line tool. The strap on the horse's face is drawn with a series of short, straight lines. The pencil tool just couldn't be held steady enough for these long lines. Note the bridle connections that were created with the pencil and eraser tools. The rein is a long arc from bit to neck.

5. You can render as many details as you have time and patience to draw, and soon you'll want to experiment with color. Before you reach for the paint bucket, however, make sure your paths of pixels that enclose the shapes you wish to color are closed shapes. Each enclosed shape must not have any pixels missing; otherwise, your color will leak to other portions of your drawing and the background.

6. Now the fun starts. The beauty of painting on a microcomputer is that you can splash color about and if you don't like it, you can undo at least your last color. If things don't work out, you can always start over. Your best strategy is to save your line drawing at various stages as separate files. That way, if you make a mistake, you can avoid having to start over completely from scratch.

7. PixelPaint offers some powerful graduated fill effects that can blend or fade colors (which you choose) and allow you to lay them down in virtually any direction. The scaled armor is filled with a range of colors from pink through dark blue through light aqua. The gold feathers on the breast plate are filled with a blend from brown to light yellow. The marbles are best rendered by a shape tool—in this case, an ellipse. Inside the circles are radial fills. The custom palette for these fills is composed of perhaps one hundred colors. All of these fill effects are handled easily, programmed by you and executed with the click of a mouse-button an the various closed shapes.

8. The nostril of the horse isn't very expressive. To work on it, the lasso tool is used to cut the piece out of the rest of the illustration so that you can modify it without wrecking what you've already created. Once you've reworked the nostril to your satisfaction, lasso it again and paste it back on the nose where it belongs.

9. It's easy to become absorbed by details at this stage of the composition. That's one of the beguiling qualities of this medium. The rein has been colored with a directional fill of aqua blended with dark green. The direction of the fill is diagonal. Also, you can begin to smudge the colors of the marbles. The smudge tool, a special effect of the paintbrush, simulates a finger smudging a blob of paint on a surface.

10. The bridle straps are directional fills of gold (the color blend from brown to light yellow). The background behind the marbles is a directional fill (upper left to lower right) of pink through purple. Working with directional rather than solid fills gives you the opportunity to render contours and form, with elements of your composition displaying highlights and shadows. The highlight on the marble is white, giving the element a glasslike quality.

11. Finis!

Gary Olsen

PAINTING TEXTURES
· ·
THE ELEPHANT

This is a study in creating textures on a computer. I realize that this may sound unusual to a traditionally trained artist. The term "texture" is something that belongs to a more tactile medium, a gessoed canvas, or an illustration board. So how do you create a texture on a computer?

First of all, you create the *illusion* of texture with the manipulation of batches of pixels. You use screen tools such as the spray can/airbrush, paintbrush, and a fill pattern effect called "tiling."

PixelPaint, a color paint program for the Macintosh, has an excellent tile effect among its tools. Most good color paint programs, regardless of the platform, have this feature. It merely allows you to create a custom pattern or random combination of color. After creating a swatch, you can paste it into your graphic using the Fill Effect command. Now your brush, bucket or spray can will color everything you wish with your custom pattern.

I've included some custom pattern swatches on these layouts to show how I recreated the effect of the elephant's rough and wrinkled skin. I first darkened the swatches for shadows and lightened them for highlights. Next, I used the bucket tool to fill the various closed-path shapes of my drawing. The brush tool can be filled with the fill effect as well as the bucket. The brush offers more control and allows you to apply the various fills to create highlights and shadows.

The icons from my program have been pasted near the areas of my drawing where they came into play, I began this graphic with a tightly rendered black line drawing. I find it easier to control the outcome by beginning this way. With a carefully rendered line drawing and shapes inclosed completely by paths of pixels, bucket fills won't escape to accidentally fill the screen. This is called a "leak," and undoing or cleaning these up wastes a lot of time.

TOOLS USED IN MAKING TEXTURES:

Direct rendering tools:
The spray can and the paintbrush are the best tools for creating multi-hued random patterns.

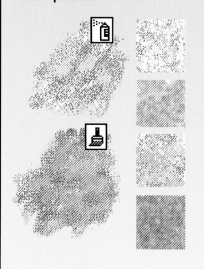

Once the desired effect is achieved, you can select a portion of the pattern with the marquee tool. Once selected, the swatch can be darkened, lightened, or softened as demonstrated later. Programs like PixelPaint allow you to copy these selected swatches into a tiling buffer that repeats the image in a continuous pattern to fill any enclosed shape. The bucket tool is used to facilitate the fill.

But before we can have fun with textures, we've got to draw something neat to texturize! We begin with the pencil tool.

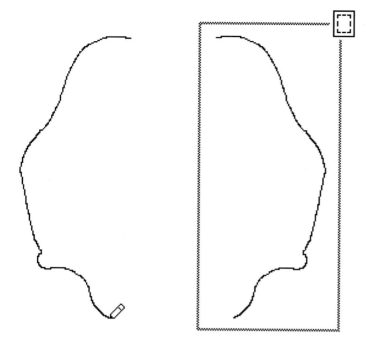

1. Draw the left half of the skull. Select the half with the marquee tool, copy it, and flip it on the horizontal. Then paste the two halves together to form the skull section.

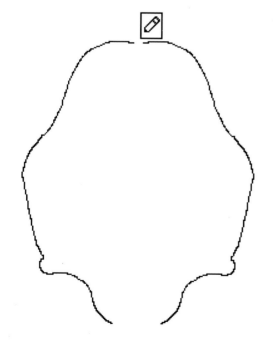

2. Continue using the pencil tool to touch up the pixel path.

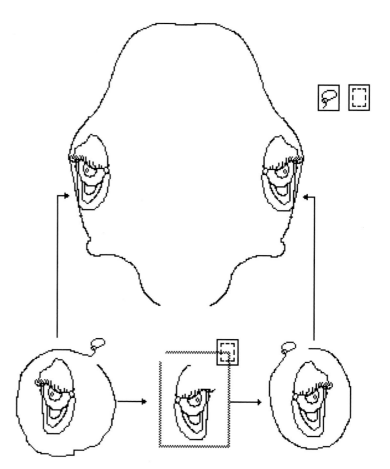

3. It's best to draw the eye off to the side, then encircle it with the lasso and move it into place. With the marquee tool, you can select the eye, make a copy of it, and flip it on the horizontal to create a mirror image. Then paste it on the other side of the head for a perfect pair of eyes only a mother elephant could love.

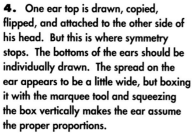

4. One ear top is drawn, copied, flipped, and attached to the other side of his head. But this is where symmetry stops. The bottoms of the ears should be individually drawn. The spread on the ear appears to be a little wide, but boxing it with the marquee tool and squeezing the box vertically makes the ear assume the proper proportions.

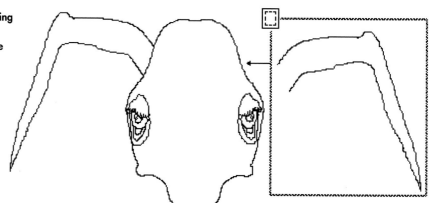

5. This step is a bit tricky. The concept here is an elephant with pencils for tusks. Tusks are drawn with the arc tool, and details rendered with the circle and straight line tools. You can do one tusk, copy and flip it, or you can draw them individually. The tips of the pencils are small circles, which can be drawn off to the side. Lasso and drag them into position. The eraser eliminates the lines you don't need.

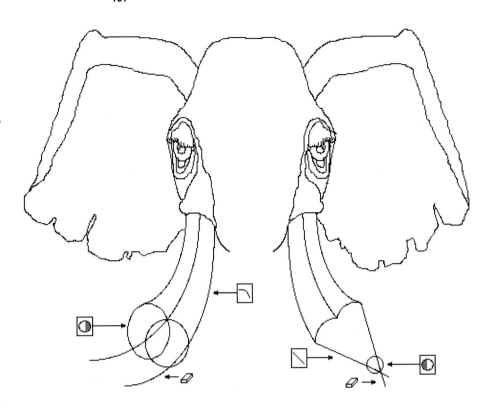

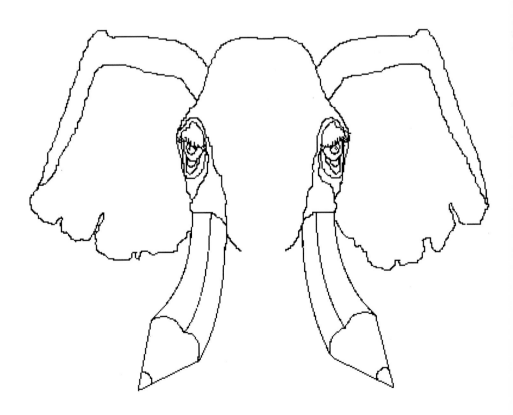

6. It's trunk time—perhaps the most difficult rendering job so far. You want to give it a nice, graceful shape. The pencil tool will give you the most control here. You'll draw over stuff you've already drawn, but that's why the eraser was invented.

7. The trunk looks a little flat. Modeling with line and color textures should save you. The tip of the trunk is drawn off to the side with the pencil, lassoed, and dragged into position. The pencil and eraser will clean up details.

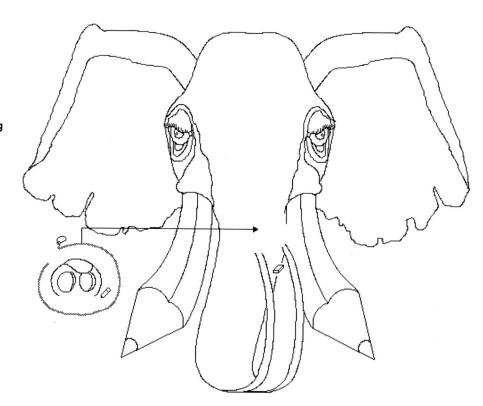

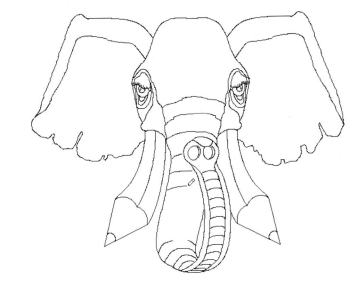

8. You now must make sure that specific areas to be filled with our colors are completely surrounded by a pixel line. Any areas you want to fill with color that have an open path, or a missing pixel, will leak color to other parts of the illustration or background.

9. You've made a significant jump to the fully drawn elephant. Based on what you've already accomplished, perhaps you have some of your own ideas on how the rest of the elephant should look. If not, this is what it's supposed to look like for this particular project. The elephant in this composition is intended to look somewhat three-dimensional, coming right at the viewer. For rendering the rest of the elephant, the best tool is the pencil.

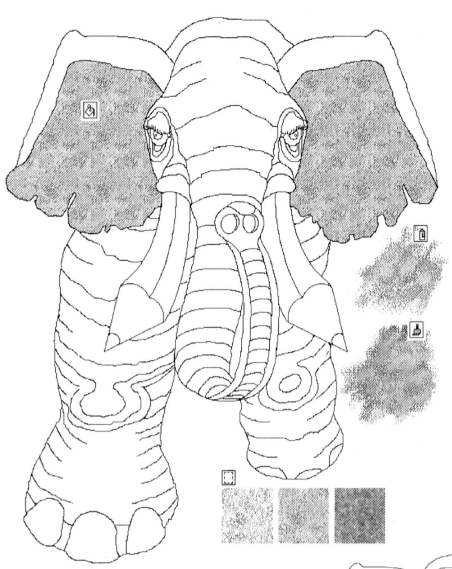

10. Paint programs like PixelPaint allow you to create your own fill patterns. In this case, it's called "tiling." You create a pattern, use the marquee tool to copy it to your clipboard, and then paste it into your tile maker. Activating the Tiling command, then, allows your paint bucket or brush to lay down a continuous tone or texture.

In this illustration, I created my tile with various shades of gray and taupe spray paint off to the side. I then smeared the pixels together using a variation of the brush tool.

The marquee tool was used to cut out swatches from my little mess. Using the Lighten, Darken and Smoothing commands, I created three different tile fills. The ears have already received a bucketful of the lighter fill pattern. The darker tones will be used with the bucket or brush to mottle the shaded areas.

11. The handiest tools for rendering the textured fills are the paint can and paintbrush. I've now created four swatches, and each will have a specific use. The darker colors are for objects farther away, the lighter textures for those I want closest to the viewer.

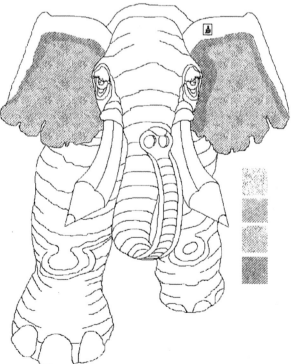

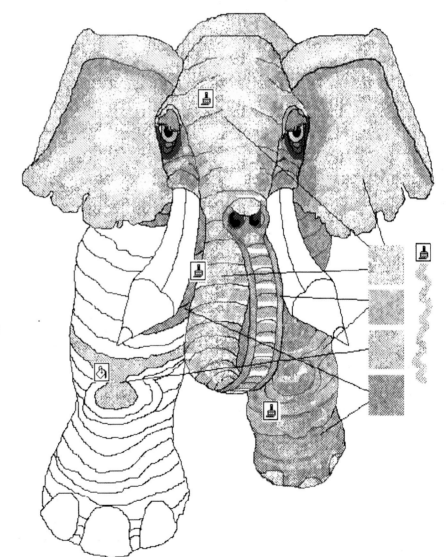

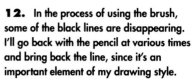

12. In the process of using the brush, some of the black lines are disappearing. I'll go back with the pencil at various times and bring back the line, since it's an important element of my drawing style.

Some of the fills are beginning to look too stepped. See the leg on the right? This is where I will go back in, using the brush filled with a lighter shade from the swatch blocks, and create a more modeled look. I even use the spray can; however, it's set on Airbrush to provide a more controlled spray to mix up the pixels a little more. You don't want to overdo it with the spray tool. It can really obliterate your line work.

13. Here's a map of where certain textures are being applied. Details around the eyes and trunk are rendered with the pencil and small brush tool. The bucket fills areas faster than the brush but the brush is best for blending, applying highlight colors, and applying color to small areas. This is where you can experiment and develop your own painting techniques.

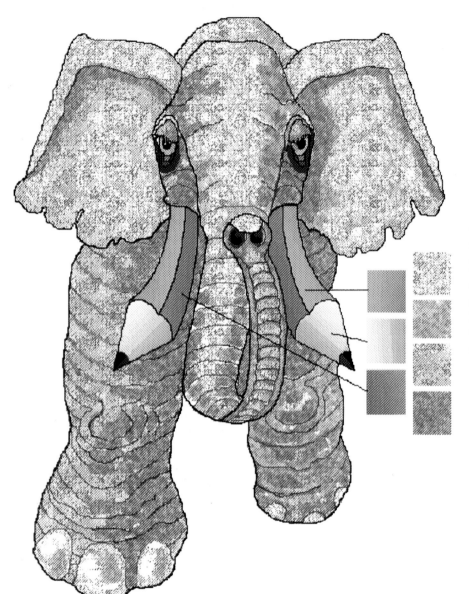

14. After you're reasonably satisfied with the texture work, use smooth graduated fills for the pencil tusks so that they contrast and project from the illustration. The color swatches for the tusks are provided. They are composed of a blend from dark orange to light yellow. Pixel-Paint, like all good paint programs, allows you to program your own color palette and blends.

15. At right is a thumbnail of the type elements and circle vignette, which was prepared in a PostScript drawing program that provided powerful type manipulation tools not available in my paint program. The drawing program enables you to run type around a circle. The paint program, thankfully, allows for importation of graphic elements from other programs. In the next step, it all comes together.

16. The type was shaded with a graduated fill that matches the colors in the pencil. Some shadowing was added. In fact, PixelPaint has an automatic shadowing command that allows you to place a drop shadow behind graphic elements just by circling them. You can also select the color or pattern you want the shadow to be. The radial blue fill within the circle was accomplished prior to pasting the elephant over the top of the circle. The "Art for Peanuts" caption is somewhat tongue-in-cheek.

HOW TO WORK WITH SERVICE BUREAUS

. . . .

Where to go when you want slides, high-resolution page layouts, color separations, color proofs and solid advice about making your work the best it can be.

Often in computer graphic production, we find ourselves not so much on the cutting edge of technology, but rather the ragged edge. Our creativity frequently tests the limitations of our equipment, and we encounter difficulties we feel no other artist or designer has experienced. The problem is that computer artists generally work on several different technical platforms, and they tend to work independently—outside the mainstream of the corporate world. At the service bureau, technicians constantly deal with designers and artists. It's probably the best place to get answers to our problems.

Most service bureaus specialize. One will be strong in four-color process and not know a thing about making color transparencies or slides. Another will have a top-of-the-line, high-resolution imagesetter and not know how to produce much more than film positives. Finding a truly all-inclusive service bureau that can handle any

. . . .
Max Seabaugh, "Car Hops 'Type to Go'"
Seabaugh illustrated an article on service bureaus for *Publish!* magazine using SuperPaint on a Macintosh.

graphic arts challenge with expertise and confidence can be a quest.

The level and quantity of the services they provide correlate to the size and sophistication of the market they serve. If you're in a big city, you've got your pick of full-service bureaus. I live in a small Midwestern town—consequently, I depend on three different service bureaus in three different cities. Each specializes in reproducing specific kinds of graphic files. My local bureau—which really isn't a service bureau but a graphics studio with a Linotronic machine—is great for desktop publishing output and some simple spot-color illustrations. Beyond that, I have to go elsewhere.

SERVICE BUREAU HARDWARE LIST
An annotated list compiled for service bureaus as well as artists.

Scanners—Gray-scale or, if you're lucky, a color scanner. A full-service operation will have both of these as well as optical character reader (OCR) software to enable you to scan pages of text into your favorite word processing program.

Laser Printer—A 300 dpi monochrome on the order of an Apple LaserWriter IINT, NTX or IIg (600 dpi) is an essential piece of equipment.

Color Laser Printer—A PostScript color printer such as a QMS ColorScript or a Tektronix is nice to have for color proofing—especially before you commit files to the more expensive process of an imagesetter.

Medium-Resolution Laser Printer—If you don't have continuous halftones or screens and just print line art and text, 600 to 1,200 dpi output on a plain paper laser printer is more than adequate. Two machines that are ideal medium-resolution printers: NewGen Turbo PS/600T (600 dpi output) and the NewGen PS/1200T. These devices can output direct to printing plate, which makes them particularly useful to small, quick print shops.

PostScript Imagesetter—The Linotronic, the Compugraphic ImageSetter, and the Optronics Color Setter 4000 can all reproduce type and images from 1,200 up to nearly 4,000 dpi on at least two types of film materials: positive paper and negative film. These machines are capable of producing high-quality film positives as well as negative process color separations.

Film Recorder—Takes raster image files and turns them into 35mm color transparencies of approximately 4,000 lines-per-inch resolu-

Mike McCulley, untitled
This three-dimensional model can be rotated at any angle. Illustrations begin as a wire-frame model over which a "skin" or surface can be stretched. Matrix QRC film recorder output is 4,000 lines-per-inch resolution.

tion for presentation graphics and some pre-press applications. Most slide makers are simple raster image processors that create high-resolution reproductions of graphics. This is a critical point, since typefaces you've used in your graphic may not be available on the film recorder; therefore, it might have to substitute typefaces. Find out just which fonts are available at your service bureau on all equipment to which you'll download your images.

Fax Machine—Used for transmitting images or data files to other bureaus or directly to clients. More important, you can use the fax yourself for transmitting reference pages to your bureau along with the computer data over a phone modem.

Phone Modem—This is an excellent device for transmitting your files to your service bureau.

High-Resolution Color Imaging System—This expensive device delivers a variety of color outputs, from presentation graphics to pre-press. Scitex, Hell, Crosfield Dicomed, Kodak Atex, ImagiTex, and Dai Nippon Screen, just to mention a few, are configured to accept computer graphics from many platforms. Some high-end systems require you to run their own proprietary graphics software on your microcomputer to access their powerful output. Others ascribe to the Open Pre-press Interface (OPI). OPI is a universal standard, established to promote compatibility of Macintosh and other microcomputer graphic platforms with high-end pre-press technology.

SOFTWARE

Your service bureau must have current versions of your graphic software, but I would caution you *not to give copies of your software to your service bureau.* All kinds of problems can result from this.

First, giving away copies of your commercial software, which includes downloadable font software, is against the law. Your copy may have been encrypted with a personalization code so that software companies can trace errant copies. This leaves the possibility that software companies will find out if your copy has been given to unauthorized users.

Another problem is that incompatible versions of the same software may corrupt one another. Not only can print drivers become corrupted and inoperable, but worse, your graphic files may be rendered inoperative and unprintable. A good service bureau avoids all of these problems by keeping their systems clean and their software versions completely current.

COMPUTER VIRUSES

Unwitting service bureaus are particularly prone to computer viruses. When you receive data disks back from a bureau, run them through an antivirus or vaccine program to make sure you don't infect your software and computer's operating system. Better yet, get a good virus detection and/or intercept program for your computer system. Several good ones are on the market, and they are easy to run.

HOW TO BE DISAPPOINTED WITH A SERVICE BUREAU'S RESULTS
The most common problems:
"Sorry, we can't read your graphic files...." Incompatible software. Your service bureau doesn't have the same software or software version number you have. You are working with more recent versions than the service bureau's. It is, however, OK to have a program that is older by a version or two than your service bureau's. They can convert your file to the new format. This is seldom risky. The

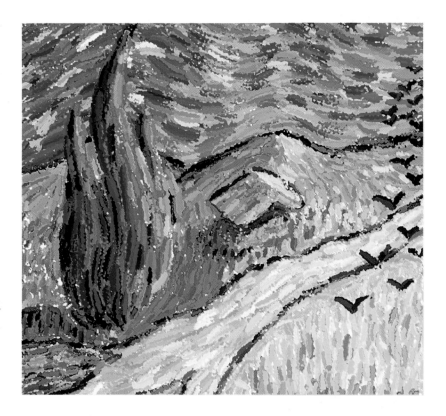

worst that can happen is that they screw up your file and you must send them another copy of your original. *Be sure to send them a copy of your graphic or document—never send the original.*
"Your type spacing is all goofed up! We can't reformat it without completely substituting your fonts with ours. Please advise us...." Incompatible font files. You used fonts that your bureau didn't have. *Advice: Get a complete printout or catalog of your service bureau's typefaces.* Also, don't use style effects in your programs to change your fonts (italic, bold, outline, etc.). These only mess up your fonts when you output to another device. Use only pure fonts, like a downloadable bold, italic or outline face. Program modifications to type are not honored by other, separate system-based image processors.
"Why is my illustration missing on my newsletter's page layout?" It was probably a TIFF image, right? You

Mark Zimmer, "Cypress Tree" Zimmer, president of Fractal Design Corporation, created this painting with Fractal Design Painter. The painting in the style of Van Gogh was produced with a cloning tool that makes this effect possible. Another tool permits you to create works in the style of Seurat.

Deb Victor, "Dance"
This was produced using Crosfield Dicomed on an IBM-AT.

didn't include the original TIFF on the same disk with your page layout file. That's an easy mistake to make. The graphic represented on the page layout is low resolution (and it takes up less memory in your document). But when it comes time to print out the page, the file needs the rest of the graphic information necessary to reproduce itself in high resolution. Include copies of your image files—EPS, PICT, PICT2—and whatever else you integrate into a document. If something should corrupt the illustration or you want to print it out separately from your document, at least the file will be on hand to manipulate or modify.

Page layout programs, like PageMaker and Quark, have some built-in image file checklists that give you a rundown of the types of image files your document is connected to. If the connection

is broken, the software will warn you that it cannot find that graphics file when you try to open the file or order it to print.

There is also some software on the market that can help you keep track of image files and fonts globally in a complex page layout document. One such program is called Checklist, which scans PageMaker and PostScript files from most Mac and several PC applications.

"Why doesn't my color key, made from my separations, match my original colors?" There are a lot of reasons this happened. Here's what you need to do:

1. Straighten out your palette. Base all of your colors on the process color or CMYK color model, which is used for four-color printing. Most artists new to the computer tend to work in RGB color. RGB (red, green, blue) is direct color produced by a cathode ray tube (computer display terminal). This color is vivid and doesn't behave like the color used in printing. Printing inks are generally transparent inks that coat a piece of paper, allowing light to reflect through and transmit color to the eye.

To avoid disappointment and attain more accurate color from display to output, convert your image (preferably while it's onscreen, or, better yet, while you are creating it) to a CMYK color model. An image-editing program (I tend to prefer Adobe Photoshop for this) does this nicely, giving you the opportunity to change from RGB (its native color model) to CMYK. You will notice immediately that CMYK is less intense on your screen and colors are somewhat darker than RGB color. This is because your graphics program is automatically compensating for the reflective nature of CMYK process color, and it's adjusting the colors for your monitor's display.

Using spot-color or Pantone is OK if you are working with spot-color jobs. Avoid using them in a four-color process job, however.

2. Recheck how you specified your inks to print in your print menu. You might have unknowingly specified certain inks to overprint. By doing this, you've laid one ink on top of another and changed the color completely. This is a problem unique to PostScript object-oriented drawing programs, where every object can be a printable element not necessarily integrated into the whole illustration. In other words, all the red objects you specified in your drawing will overprint any object that lies beneath them if you want them to. If you don't want to overprint the ink, the object beneath will form "cutouts" so the red doesn't overprint on the underlying colors.

3. Calibrate for color accuracy. Various steps in your hardware chain, which includes your computer and your service bureau's computer and output devices, must be regularly calibrated to deliver accurate color and quality results.

First, regularly calibrate your computer's display monitor. Most important, calibrate it in the ambient studio light conditions during which you will do most of your work. If you have image-editing software (Photoshop, for example), it includes a gamma correction program that can help you

Philip Rodriguez, "Type Faces"
Created using Micrografx Designer on the PC.

Laura Lamar, untitled
This label design for Nunes Farms was prepared using Adobe Illustrator, Aldus FreeHand, and Letraset Ready, Set, Go! on a Macintosh.

adjust your monitor to compensate for ambient light levels in your work area. Check your program's documentation for specifics. Don't ignore this important capability of your software. If you're going to produce quality results, you must be conscientious about color accuracy.

Also, your computer's color circuit board likely came with software to help you balance your monitor's vertical and horizontal registration—convergence, white balance and other monitor characteristics. It doesn't require a professional to do these things, unless, of course, your computer has problems that cannot be resolved by the basic adjustments.

Rather expensive accessory monitor calibration devices and software are on the market, most of which use a suction-cup sensor that sticks to your screen and reads the results of onscreen testing rou-

tines and automatically adjusts your monitor's in-board controls. Unless you're involved in graphic design jobs that require absolutely precise color management, you can do without these devices until you get more advanced.

Your service bureau should calibrate its computers and output devices to deliver accuracy of color and proper negative or positive densities. Also, its film processing equipment should be kept in top shape. A conscientious service bureau calibrates its equipment on a frequent and regular basis (at least once a week). You can't control how often your service bureau calibrates its equipment, but you can refuse to accept bad film separations. You should be able to ask the right questions to help resolve the problems.

My color seps didn't print! Check your print options menu to see if all the colors are turned on.

I got spot-color separations and cyan, magenta, yellow and black separations! I've got four pieces of film I didn't ask for and I must pay for them! Some software programs still give you the choice in the print options menu to specify spot color or process color. If you don't shut off the CMYK colors, they may print. One of the last things you do before sending a file to a printing device (especially a PostScript device from which separations are made) is to check which inks are printing and which ones you do not want.

My printer says he can't hold registration on my spot-color illustration prepared in Aldus FreeHand because I didn't specify traps and chokes. What are they? Traps and chokes are covered in the documentation of your software. In fact, Aldus has a booklet (*Aldus FreeHand and Commercial Printing*) on how to deal with commercial printers' trap and choke requirements, and it's included with every program. This is the best documentation I've read

on working with printers and service bureaus.

A trap is used when you try to spread the edges of a lighter element against a darker background. You accomplish this by slightly overlapping (called "overprinting" in FreeHand) the element's outline to prevent white space from peeking around the edges if the plates on the press are slightly misaligned. A choke is used to trap a dark element on a light background. You specify the outline of the darker object to be the same color as the background. Depending on the complexity of your illustration, of course, it should be easy to specify trapping. Get into the habit of doing it as you prepare your illustration and avoid having to go in later to make traps and chokes.

Why all the bother? Shouldn't the press operator be more vigilant? Registration problems are not caused by a less-than-conscientious press operator . Misregistration is a real problem, especially with large-size printing jobs, as the paper stretches or shrinks slightly between applications of ink due to moisture. Paper is like a sponge, and a slightly higher humidity causes it to swell. To compensate for this potential for misalignment, you should create traps and chokes right in your illustration.

In FreeHand, Micrografx Designer, CorelDRAW and Adobe Illustrator, trapping can be done as you create your illustration by specifying the overprinting of lines that comprise your drawing. Letters or large type elements can also be trapped.

While many printing or separating problems may be caused at least in part by the creator of the graphic, two problems are most often caused at the service bureau:

Deb Victor, "Fan and Cherry Blossoms"
Victor created this illustration using Crosfield Dicomed on an IBM-AT.

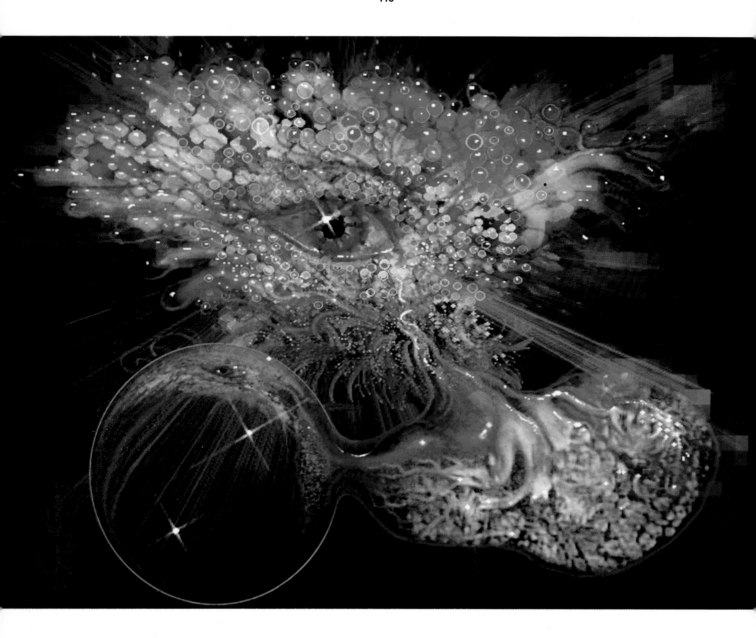

Jim Thompson, "The Eye"
Jim output this to a film processor from his state-of-the-art PC.

1. My Linotronic negatives have tiny pinholes of light showing through, or my film positives have tiny black specs on them. Is it something I did? No. This problem has nothing to do with computer equipment or software. It's dirty film processing equipment. What you see is the result of broken crusts of crystallized developer that break free of the roller mechanisms and stick to the film and transport rollers. Or, it's just plain dirt.

2. My type is so thin in places it's barely readable. It looks good onscreen, so what's the problem? This is a chemical developer or a photographic film or paper problem. Contact your service bureau; let the technician know that the quality of the output was not acceptable.

A full-color illustration I had prepared for process color output (CMYK) was printed and the color proof reveals a moiré pattern (an undesirable rosette pattern visible in the continuous tonal areas). How can I or my service bureau eliminate this? To eliminate this patterning requires an approach that will attain as fine a dot pattern as

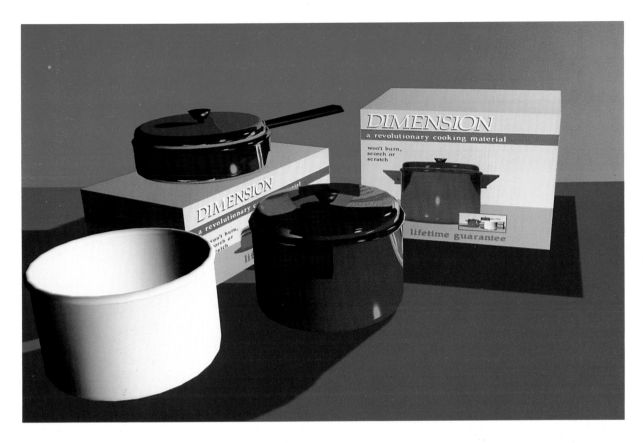

This artwork was produced in AT&T Graphics Software Labs. Work is created on extremely advanced turnkey systems that use a personal computer as the input device. As advanced as these systems might seem, they still incorporate the same object-oriented, onscreen drawing and painting tools as the off-the-shelf computers. Output on these advanced systems is usually intended for high-end applications like video production, color film for publishing, or slide presentations. Output is done at an authorized dealer service bureau.

possible (i.e., as high a resolution as possible) in your image.

Your image must be prepared at the highest resolution possible, based on this simple formula: 2 x intended lpi = dpi. In other words, determine your image's resolution (dots per inch) by at least doubling your lpi (lines per inch). Lpi is the measurement standard of the color printing trade, and it is not the same as dpi, the resolution measurement of the computer graphics industry. All color-imaging illustration and design programs have dpi and lpi measurement settings that you can specify. So before you begin an illustration, ask yourself, what is the final destination for this graphic file? If it will be published, what are the capabilities of the press on which it will be printed?

Most commercial printing presses that do color require at least 133 lpi images for best results. Some presses have even higher lpi han-

dling capabilities. The fact is, and this can't be repeated enough, the higher the resolution, the fewer problems you will have with moiré and unwanted tonal patterning.

FILE COMPRESSION

File compression is absolutely essential when transporting or transmitting your graphic files, particularly over telephone lines via modem. Think about transmitting a 5 megabyte file over a modem. Even at 9,600 baud, it could take an eternity, and time is money. But with file compression, you can shrink the file down to less than half its original size, decreasing the time it takes to transmit.

Using a compression program can be an excellent way to free up space on your hard disk. Also, a squeezed file can fit on a floppy where it might have been too big to fit before. It's also a good way to store backup files of your important graphics and data.

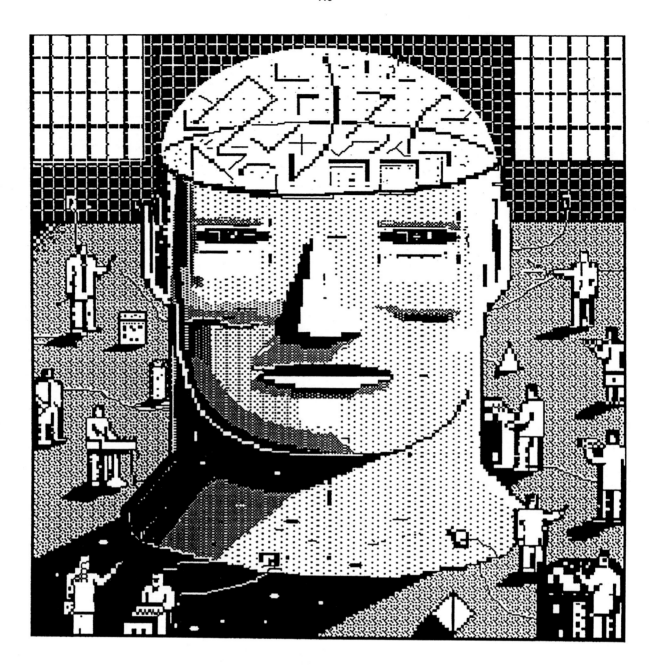

Max Seabaugh, "Artificial Intelligence"
Seabaugh produced this illustration using SuperPaint on a Macintosh.

Of course you must extract the files from their compact state if you are to use them. You can't leave TIFF files compacted while their destination page layout file opens or is sent to a printer. The document must find these files, and it won't if they're compacted in a Stuffit archive. Unstuffing files doesn't take long, however. Don't worry; there is no degradation of the file data as a result of being stuffed and extracted.

Some types of files compress better than others. Text and number data files compact extremely well, to almost 25 percent of their original size. But complex bit-map graphics, scanned photographs and high-resolution bit-map images contain more data that can't be crunched easily. Therefore, bit-map files compress less radically than other types, such as PostScript drawing files.

Two file compression programs

that have wide circulation among service bureaus and user groups are Stuffit (i.e., Stuffit Deluxe, Stuffit Pro) and Compact Pro. Although these are available as shareware, you should obtain registered copies with complete documentation.

Stuffit software has been around a long time. Originally developed for the Mac community as shareware by Raymond Lau, virtually everybody in computer graphics now uses it. Service bureaus have it so you should encounter no problem unpacking your compacted Stuffit files.

Compact Pro, developed by Bill Goodman, is gaining in popularity, however, probably because it allows you to create self-opening

archives that don't require the destination computer to have the program. At this writing, Stuffit requires the destination computer to have the Stuffit program to unpack files.

Your graphics programs may contain their own compression tools. Of course they are limited to saving files in their native format. This usually appears as the option Save as Compressed File in the Save menus. Image-editing software allows you to compress images you may save as TIFFs. Also, most drawing and painting programs that save to TIFF allow you to compress the file in a self-extracting format. Built-in compression doesn't affect a file's ability to be placed and displayed in

Mike McCulley, untitled
This glass head illustration was created by St. Louis-based McCulley, who works with an IBM-AT and Matrix QCR film recorder. His program is Panasonic's StudioWorks. Graphic elements begin as a wireframe model.

**Max Seabaugh,
"Self-Promotion Piece"**
Created with Adobe Illustrator on a
Macintosh II.

another document, nor does it
affect its ability to print.

HOW SERVICE BUREAUS CHARGE
**How to factor those charges
into the asking price for your
artwork or design.**

You've got to shop around. An
eight-page newsletter can cost $36
at one bureau and $136 at another
place across town. You need to
find out what a bureau charges and
how it charges. Here's what to ask:
**Do you charge per hour, per image or
both?** Certain output devices take
a long time to output an image. At
some bureaus, time is money.
Because files submitted to a service
bureau can seldom be download-
ed into a device without some preview and modification (the bureau
technician doesn't want to waste
time on stuff that doesn't at least
look good on the screen), preparation time may or may not be fac-
tored into the per-page rate.
Straight type prints quickly. Illustrations take more time. Imagesetter rates are determined by a
number of factors:

1. Number of pages—Ask when the
multiple page discount kicks in.
2. Type or art? A page of type prints
faster than graphics, so it should
be cheaper.
3. Page size—Since raster image
processors can print on various
sizes of paper (they print on continuous roll film), an 11- by-17-inch
tabloid page will cost more than
a letter-size page. If you print an
illustration on an 8$\frac{1}{2}$- by-11-inch
sheet with full bleed and you want
registration marks and overlay
labels, you will pay for the larger
sheet size.
4. Film negative or positive? Negatives are more expensive, but then
you eliminate an intermediate step
in getting your art to print.
**What's your policy on mistakes and do-
overs?** If the bureau is at fault for
poor quality, it will likely redo

pages upon request. Ask for a copy of its redo policy. Some bureaus, however, just supply the equipment and no expertise or adequate counseling. If there are do-overs, you may have to pay for them no matter what. If this is the case, find another bureau or open one yourself that is fair to artists, designers and desktop publishers. You'll run this so-called service bureau out of business in a month.

How and what do you charge for rush service? You could be charged anywhere from 25 to 200 percent over the existing rate for overnight or same-day service. Several bureaus operate a night shift to run out files.

Would you please send me your rate card? You shouldn't accept rate schedules over the phone. Be wary of ballpark price quotes and hidden charges.

Who is the person at your bureau most familiar with how your systems work with commercial printing? May I speak to him or her?

Package design, complete with product, created on an AT&T computer-based graphics system using Topas software.

CREATING AN ILLUSTRATION FROM A SCANNED IMAGE

A MEDICAL ILLUSTRATION

A cardiovascular surgeon needed a simple drawing of the lower extremity arterial system. He had a brochure illustration he liked, but it had too much detail. Our system is Macintosh, an inexpensive scanner, a monochrome paint program—Zedcor's DeskPaint and SuperMac's PixelPaint, a color paint program. DeskPaint has a unique auto-trace tool that PixelPaint does not; PixelPaint has color and DeskPaint does not. A perfect match!

Your objective is to create two different graphics of the same subject. The first will be a high-resolution line drawing that can be printed on the office laser printer for inclusion in the patient's record. The second graphic will be a colorful screen representation that the doctor can use in instructional situations, like showing the patient planned surgical procedures. Listed below is your strategy:

• Scan the original graphic and import it in DeskPaint. Actually, any monochrome paint program that accepts scanned images will do nicely. However, DeskPaint has a handy auto-trace tool that converts bit-map image into high-resolution line drawing.

• Modify the graphic to the surgeon's specifications, eliminating unnecessary detail from the scanned image.

• Auto-trace the image and export it in to a draw program (DeskDraw, a companion program to DeskPaint) for conversion to a PICT file. The line drawing can now be included in a page-layout program like PageMaker or QuarkXPress and output to a laser printer.

• Export the original revised bit-map image to PixelPaint for coloring.

THE TOOLBOX:

DeskPaint's toolbox follows the classic Macintosh user interface—friendly and emperically obvious. The tools that will be the most useful during this project are given below.

The following are rendering tools—
Pencil: For freehand drawing and pixel editing.
Eraser: Erases black pixels under the eraser. The size is adjustable.
Paintbrush: Paints black, white, and patterns. The size and shape is adjustable.
Paint bucket: Fills an enclosed path of pixels with solid black or a fill pattern.

The following are image select tools—
Lasso: Selects only the graphic and white areas enclosed by pixels for movement, manipulation, copying, pasting, and deleting.
Marquee box: Selects rectangular areas for movement, manipulation, copying, pasting, and deleting.
Zoom tool: This will help us immensely. Sometimes called "fatbits" we can get down to the pixel level for precise editing.

Auto-tracing tool: By touching this tool on various bit-map shapes, the program automatically traces them for cutting and pasting to a drawing program for high-resolution printing.

1. First, make a line-art scan (right) and open the scanned image in your paint program. Note the line down the middle. That's the page gutter from the brochure. You only need to work on one leg since we have the ability to copy, paste and flip the revised art to make a symmetrical pair. For now, take your marquee box, and select and remove the right half of the illustration.

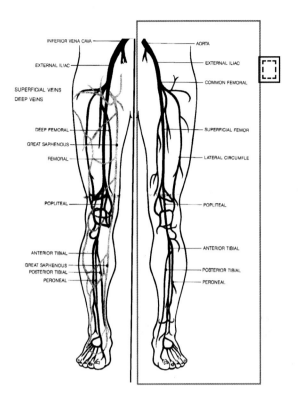

2. Your primary tools for cleanup are the pencil and eraser. You need to eliminate a lot of detail, so the zoom tool will help get you close for pixel-by-pixel editing. Just click on the area you want larger, and you're there in an instant.

3. You cleaned up the graphic pretty well. The doctor wanted to lengthen the aorta at the top, separate the three vessels below the knee, and widen the vessels overall to allow drawing details, like arterial blockages, in the vessels themselves. You will need to trace those vessels, an excellent opportunity for the auto-trace tool. For now, the tracery of vessels can remain black. They'll trace better when you are ready. The paintbrush is handy for thick lines you may have omitted or need to modify.

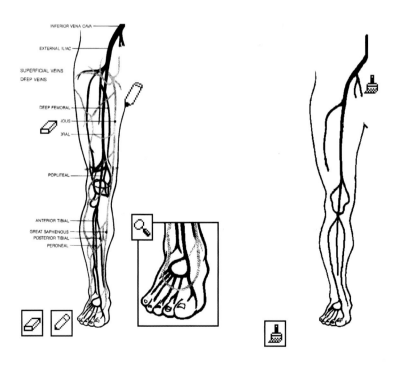

4. Now copy and flip the leg for a perfectly matched pair. Surround the graphic with the marquee tool. Copy it and command the program to flip the new image on a horizontal plane. It can then be moved next to its reflected image to complete the symmetrical graphic.

5. If you're lucky, the pieces will line up nicely, but you might have to revert to the pencil to patch up lines and other details. Line integrity is important in preparing the graphic for auto-tracing.

The next step involves saving your graphic in the right format. Before you auto-trace your finished bit-map illustration, make a copy of it in a format compatible with your color paint program. In this case, MacPaint is the most appropriate format. PixelPaint will open MacPaint formatted files. Under the file menu, do a "Save As..." and you will be given some available format choices in which to save your document. A shortcut might be to use your system software's clipboard or scrapbook, but that can be risky and, in some circumstances, you may lose your illustration. Just save the painting as an editable document. You might need it again in its native format to make changes.

6. With DeskPaint's auto-trace tool, you merely have to touch the lines or shapes you want traced, and the program does it. You then must copy the trace to your system's clipboard.

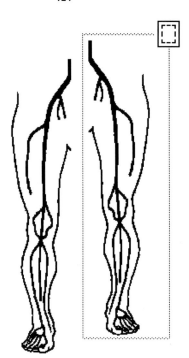
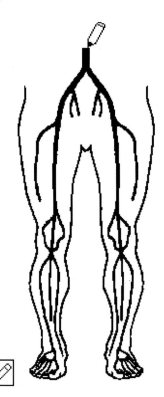

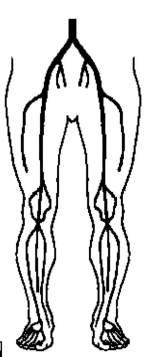

7. The surgeon looks at the drawing at this point and decides he wants more details removed to make the graphic even simpler. Good thing you saved the original bit-map! After additional changes, auto-trace again. The left image is the auto-traced line drawing executed in your original paint program. Once in the draw program, the line drawing can be further modified; that is, the lines can be moved about in typical drafting program fashion. Your objective in the draw program is to create a file compatible with laser printer output.

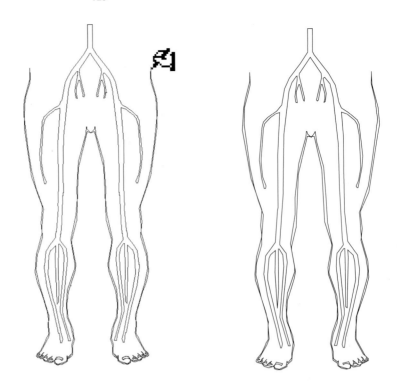

8. Since this graphic's primary function will be as an onscreen demonstration graphic and possibly a patient record if the surgeon should ever obtain a color printer, cutting and pasting the line drawing into PixelPaint will enable you to render a fast color comp. Coloring the shapes with the paint bucket and selected palette colors goes quickly. The tools are the same as in any monochrome paint program. Touch-ups and the arterial blockage were rendered with the brush tools. The flesh color was poured into the closed path of pixels, created first using the brush filled with flesh-colored paint at the top where there were no black lines. Finally, the text tool facilitated adding the captions. The lines were drawn by the straight line tool.

9. This caption box is simple. Just select a portion of the graphic with the marquee tool, enlarge it, and put a shadow box around it. Use the brush to render any detail colors.

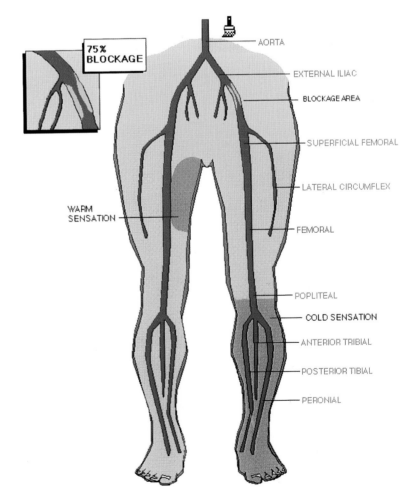

EDITING AND MANIPULATING
PHOTOGRAPHIC IMAGES

Creating art with image-editing/manipulating programs.

As personal computers have become more powerful and certainly more colorful, artists and designers have discovered they can do much more than render interesting images using painting and drawing programs. Photographic image manipulation, a technology that was once the domain of the high-end proprietary workstation environment, or practiced by those mysterious color separation houses, is now available for a relatively modest investment in a scanner and off-the-shelf software.

The photographic image has been an important tool for artists and illustrators since the camera was invented. But combine the photograph with the capabilities of the computer, and you have invented a new, more sophisticated art form. Some computer artists even specialize in photo manipulation; you'll see the work on several pages of this book.

Image-editing programs have often been referred to as digital darkrooms. They can certainly han-

dle many of the tasks that once were relegated to an enlarger and chemicals. For example, if an image is underexposed, scan it into the computer, lighten it, adjust the contrast, refine the color balance and print it. It's that simple if you have a scanner and image-editing software.

But if you think these programs are strictly for photo retouching or manipulation, you may be limiting yourself. I know of artists who use this software as their primary painting program. And why not? They utilize the complete palette of over 16 million colors. They have tools identical to those found in painting programs, and image-editing programs offer some painting features that aren't available in more traditional paint programs.

Celebrated Mac artist Bert Monroy is one of these artists, and he wrote the book (literally) on Photoshop (_The Official Adobe Photoshop Handbook_). Artists have also discovered the brush, airbrush and finger blend tools to be much more versatile and precise in photo manipulation programs.

At the time of this writing, several software packages are available on both Macintosh and PC platforms. Among the most popular are Adobe Photoshop (Adobe Systems), and Color Studio (Fractal Design) for the

Macintosh; and Adobe Photoshop PC, Picture Publisher (Micrografx), PhotoStyler (Aldus) and Publisher's Paintbrush (ZSoft) for the PC. They all operate similarly in that they enable the user to select a portion of a scanned or digitized image, and manipulate the pixels that make up this image into a new one of the artist's making. All incorporate a number of tools and filters for special effects and output to laser printers, slides and high-end, pre-press color systems.

DIGITIZING AN IMAGE

To better understand image editing, it helps to have a basic understanding of what happens to an image when it is digitized or scanned. Basically, digitizing a traditional (or analog) image is converting it into bytes, bits and pixels. These are the basic building blocks of your computer image. Grouped together, they form a rectangular grid called a pixelmap (or bit-map). Pixelmaps aren't new, nor are they exclusive to computer graphics. Weavers, embroiderers and cross-stitch artisans have been using pixelmaps (or rectangular matrixes) for more than a thousand years.

On a computer pixelmap, each square of the pixelmap is plotted with an integer X and Y value. Each

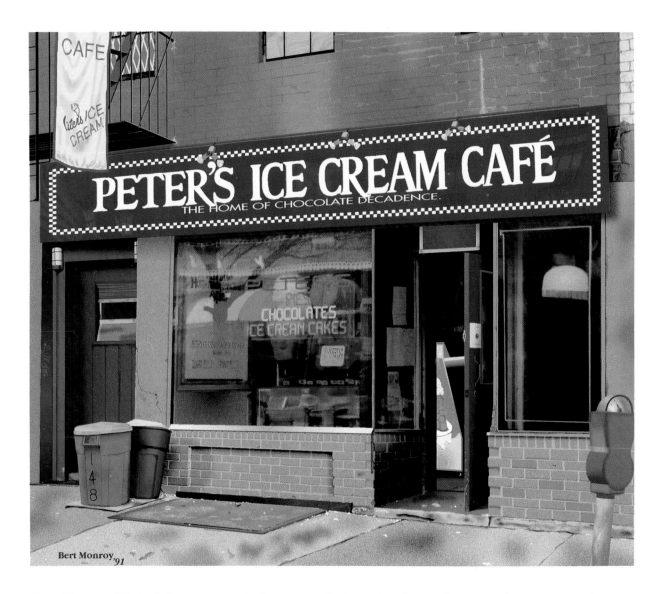

Bert Monroy '91

Bert Monroy, "Peter's Ice Cream Café"

Monroy created this image using Adobe Illustrator and Photoshop. This photorealistic image was created with no photographic scans of any kind; the artist uses Photoshop almost exclusively as his primary paint program.

pixel represents the intensity value of that area of the image. On a simple one-bit computer display, each pixel on a pixelmap is either on or off (displayed as white or black). Working with full color on a computer is a little more complex, but the principle is the same. When you paint or retouch a photograph or other image on your computer, you use light as your medium.

Optimum Resolution

Working with scanners and photo image-editing programs requires an understanding of how to gain optimal resolution for your images. Scanning an image at the right dpi

for output clarity is essential, especially when designing or illustrating for print. If you select a dpi number that is too low, your photo will look coarse and pixelated when it's output to an imagesetter or other printing device. It will have the jagged edges that many refer to as the "jaggies." Pick a number too high, and you'll be wasting disk space on picture information you may not need and a file so large it takes most of the day to display on your computer screen. (OK, maybe I'm exaggerating just a little.)

Seriously, higher resolution files require a lot of memory to display and a lot of disk space to store. They

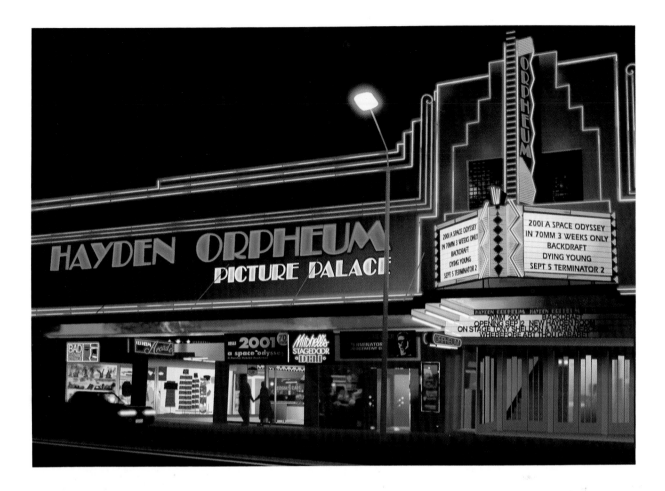

Bert Monroy, "Picture Palace"
This image was created using Adobe Illustrator and Photoshop. Monroy literally wrote the book on Photoshop, co-authoring *The Official Adobe Photoshop Handbook.*

also render more slowly and are difficult to transport from one computer to another or to an imaging device. Your aim should be to produce a clear and precise image, with a minimum amount of memory. With this in mind, consider the following when determining how to best scan and work with an image:

• What does my client need and want? Is it slides? Is it published art? If so, what size will the final image be? What resolution will my client require?

• What is the resolution capability of my output device? Will it be a laser printer (with an output of 300 to 1,200 dpi)? Will it be a Linotronic or a Compugraphic with resolutions of 1,270 to nearly 4,000 dpi? Will it be a color printer—color laser, ink jet, wax transfer, die transfer, continuous tone or high-end color printer—and at what resolu-

tion (low, medium or high)? Does the output device support the page-description language I'm working in (PostScript, Quick Draw or HPGL)?

• How will I store this image, and on what? What is the most practical resolution for the memory capacity of my computer? Will my storage or transport device be compatible with that of my client or service bureau?

You'll obviously need to confer with whomever you work with before you begin to consider the right dpi for scanning and outputting your final image.

WHICH DPI IS BEST?

Beyond decisions that are appropriate to a specific job or situation, there are some general rules to follow when determining which dpi is best. For one thing, input reso-

Original scan in color

Converted to gray scale

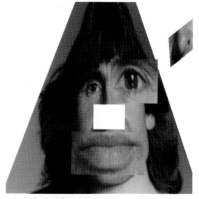

Distorting selected pieces

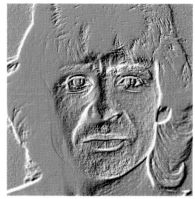

Emboss

Posterized and colorized

Changed eye color and enlarged nose

The many faces of an image-editing program. These are just a sampling of some of the things you can do to alter an image. The face actually belongs to Davy Jones of Monkees fame. These photographs were of a book project I was working on for him.

Cloned eyebrows to create moustache

Posterize—four levels

lution needn't be as high as your output resolution. High-resolution scans serve no practical purpose and take up disk space.

If you're scanning a 10-by-10-inch image into your computer that will ultimately be printed at 5-by-5-inches, scan it in at 100 percent of its size, at a resolution of 150 dpi. When you're done working with it in your image-editing program, output this image at its final size of 5-by-5-inches (50 percent of the original size) and it will be at 300 dpi, an acceptable level of clarity and a resolution level comparable to most laser printers. This way you're working with an image file that requires less memory, but you're outputting at a dpi that will render the clarity you need at a higher resolution.

And don't worry about working with a jagged 150 dpi image on your screen. Your imaging software displays your photo at the precise size you want it to be. A 300 dpi color image looks just the same on your screen as a 72 dpi image; in fact, your screen displays all images at 72 dpi.

Here's another way to determine the best scanning and output resolution: Start with the resolution level of your output device. Most commercial printers print halftones and screened color separations at 133 lines-per-inch (lpi). (This standard of measure has been around since the dawn of photoengraving, before computers and dots-per-inch. Your image-editing and page-layout software programs give you the opportunity to set your image's lpi in either the image-editing or print menu.) Ask your client and/or printer which lpi they prefer, then double this number when setting the dpi scanning resolution of your image. Scan and work with an image size of 100 percent. If your output needs to be 133 lpi, your dpi on the original scan should be set at 266 dpi.

Where precise detail is impor-

tant, such as a retouched photograph, you'll need this high resolution. But in many graphic applications, you may not need to output an image at a high resolution. If you are attempting a more painterly look, go for a lower resolution and save disk space (as well as random access memory and virtual memory to use for displaying and manipulating). You can often get away with minimum resolutions such as 72 dpi for a continuous tone image that will appear on television or for any other nonprinted visual need.

A final note on economizing disk space: When saving a TIFF scan, save your file in a compressed for-

Catherine Schmeltz and Crit Warren, "CSCA Call for Entries"
Schmeltz and Warren created this inexpensive, one-color Call for Entries for the Columbus, Ohio, Society of Communicating Arts with Digital Darkroom and PageMaker. It uses laserwriter printouts for the pictures in the finished art. The multipanel brochure was proofed as tiles on a Laserwriter NTX and was output as film negatives from lino.

Alan Brown, opera poster
Brown created three images in Photoshop for this poster. The model was shot as a silhouette against a white background. That slide was projected onto a canvas background and shot again, then scanned for use on the computer. A photo of flowers was scanned and combined with the shot of the model. The same photo of flowers was also screened back and used at the bottom of the poster.

IMAGE-EDITING TOOLS: THE BASICS

Whether it's image-editing software on a Mac or on a PC, the most popular applications use extremely similar onscreen tools. Look and feel is becoming so universal, the only difference between platforms anymore is price. Tools such as the Marquee, Ellipse and Lasso in Photoshop select pixels in much the same way as Color Studio, Painter, Aldus SuperPaint, PC Paintbrush or Publisher Paintbrush. However, there are some significant differences in how some tools perform, and each program has its own set of unique features and functions. (For example, Photoshop offers alpha channels for isolating and saving designated portions of an image.) But let's go through the tools that are basic to the operation of each.

Select Tools: Lasso, Marquee and Ellipse. These select tools allow you to select portions of the image you are working with. You can select an area of your image, lighten, darken, sharpen, blur, pixellate or modify the color without affecting the rest of the picture. You can also distort, skew, scale and change the perspective of the selected portion of the image.

The Lasso tool allows you to select a freeform group of pixels by tracing the tool over the portion of the picture you want to select. The Marquee tools select square or elliptical sections of various aspect ratios depending on how you drag your mouse or stylus diagonally across an image area.

PRECISION SELECTING

If you try to select an object by tracing its contours with the Lasso tool, you'll be cursing and complaining to yourself as a consequence of its imprecision. Don't sweat it. There are other ways of isolating a precise area.

In some programs, precision selection tools (in Photoshop it's a

mat. It will not affect the overall image quality and will likely cut the file size by as much as 50 percent. Much progress has been made and will continue to be made in image file compression. As computer artists become more demanding, we hope file sizes and compression standards will make file management easier.

pen) will enable you to select an area and convert it to Bézier curves that can be tugged to conform to the outline of an exact area. Other programs make this capability accessible through similar tools or through key commands.

In Photoshop the pen tool can be a real aid in photo retouching. Let's say you have an object that needs to be delineated from its background. You don't have the time or inclination to change the background, but want to render a thin, light-colored line around your object to subtly set it apart from its background. By using this tool you can create an anti-aliased line that will blend itself with adjoining pixels.

FEATHERING AND DEFRINGING EDGES

A selected image area has an inherently sharp and irregular edge, resembling something that was cut with dull scissors. But image-editing programs allow you to feather or defringe the edges of a pasted image. Feathering creates a gradual transition between the pixels in the selected object and the background on which it is placed. The feathering of edge pixels can even be programmed to your specifications, measured in pixel widths. This is an extremely useful tool when combining different images into a single image or picture.

Defringing is similar to feathering, but it is more precise. It can come in handy if you have positioned a selected image on a completely different colored background, and upon closer inspection you notice that you picked up some pixels along the edge of your object that contain some color from the old background. The Defringe command analyzes the colors along the edge of an image and replaces the fringe pixels containing the old background colors with the new background color.

Sharon Steuer, "Porcupine"
Sharon painted this illustration in Color-Studio with a pressure-sensitive tablet. She is not only a terrific artist, but a very astute colorist, making full use of her computer's color capabilities.

Sergio Spada, "The Scream"
Created in Photoshop.

THE MAGIC WAND TOOL

This is another kind of select tool. When I first used it, I was convinced that it was magic! Touch the wand on an area of pixels, and all adjoining "like pixels" become selected. You can change the value or color of a group of like pixels. By touching the wand on the pixel area you wish to modify, the adjoining similar pixels are automatically selected. Now you can make choices that will affect these pixels in the Filter and Select menus. You can also create masks that can be transported from one image to another. By reducing the image to two or three contrast levels with the Posterize command, the pixel groups become easier to capture for a mask.

THE RUBBER STAMP OR CLONING TOOL

The handiest tool, by far, is the Rubber Stamp (as it's called in Photoshop) or the Cloning Tool (as it's referred to in other programs). In ColorStudio, the cloning is accomplished with the Airbrush or Pencil tools. Its basic function is to repeat or clone continuous tones, patterns or entire objects from one area of an image to another. You "load" this tool with pixels in one area and transfer what you've loaded into a new area of your image.

This is a great way to retouch. For example, if you want to remove an item within a continuous tone, texture or difficult blend, your first instinct would be to match the color of the surrounding area and airbrush the object out. Why bother when you can clone an area and paint it over the offending object? It's faster, and in many cases the results are more realistic. If you remove a wrinkle by smudging or airbrushing, it may render an absolutely flawless, poreless complexion that would look artificial. Use the Cloning or Rubber Stamp tool to remove the wrinkle and you'll get better results.

THE SMUDGE TOOL

This tool simulates the effect of a finger being dragged through wet paint. It has been very popular in color painting programs. For example, a little nick on the edge of a newly placed element can be repaired quickly by merely smudging the pixels. You can smudge away a hard edge or irregular contour this way, an application that is extremely useful in retouching portraits, where you may want to obscure a blemish or two. You can also create some interesting painterly effects on a photograph with this tool.

CROPPER, GRABBER, ZOOM, PANNING AND SHARPENING TOOLS

These tools are similar to those found in Mac- and Windows-based paint programs. The Cropper tool lets you select part of an image, discarding the rest. Cropping out areas of images you don't need can reduce file sizes dramatically. The Grabber allows you to move images larger than your open window or screen. The Zoom tool allows you to magnify your image or push it into the distance. The Panning tool allows you to move back and forth, across an image area.

The Sharpening tool allows you to enhance the focus, or blur an image by increasing or decreasing the contrast of the pixels in the area you have selected.

RENDERING TOOLS: PENCIL, BRUSH, AIRBRUSH AND ERASER

The Pencil tool varies from one program to the next. In Photoshop it renders hard-edged lines and is the tool you'll probably use the least. In ColorStudio, it functions as a cloning tool.

The Paintbrush is particularly effective when retouching images. In fact, rather than use an eraser, which scrubs pixels away and leaves a hard edge, the Paintbrush, charged

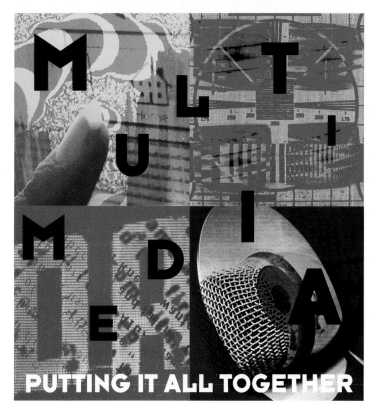

Write as Rain: WordPerfect's Online Aid–p. 22

Waste Not, Want In?–p. 27

Armchair Aviators Unite–p. 36

COMPUSERVE MAGAZINE

JANUARY 1992 $2.50

MULTIMEDIA

PUTTING IT ALL TOGETHER

with white, often makes a much better eraser--especially in tight places.

The Airbrush is a programmable paint sprayer, laying down color in soft, diffused layers.

The Eraser removes pixels down to the background color.

ADDING COLOR, LINE RENDERING AND TYPE

The Straight Line tool is more than just a line-rendering tool; it's an effective retouching tool. In a photograph, you can use it to delineate objects that may be obscured slightly against a background. You can also use it to make lines and arrows for visual aids.

Catherine Schmeltz and Crit Warren, *CompuServe* magazine cover illustration
The illustration was created in Photoshop and output as film.

Michael Johnson, untitled
This painting, used as a Christmas self-promotion, is composed of many separate photographic elements that have been manipulated and recombined into a photorealistic composition with Photostyler on a PC. Johnson feels that this new medium allows him to use elements of light to paint an illusion of actual light.

One of the most time-saving tools is the Eyedropper/Paint Sampler tool. Imagine trying to mix a color to match an area on your image you would like to retouch. Even with a computer, this would be a tedious, time-consuming task. Just place the Eyedropper on the area of the image you wish to match and, bingo! It loads this color into your foreground color box.

The Type tool integrates type elements into your image by enabling the user to compose text, select a font and indicate point size, leading and spacing. When working in Photoshop, make sure you click on "anti-aliasing" in the style menu to ensure that the letters will be smooth in your composition. And don't overlook some of the creative distortions, perspective renderings and other special effects you can apply to type in this program.

Needless to say, each block of type or character can be colored solid or with a gradient fill.

CONTROLLING COLOR

In Photoshop the Color Picker window shows two boxes that exhibit your foreground and background colors. (The smaller box is your foreground color, while the larger box outlining it is the background color.) Other programs, such as ColorStudio, show a palette and provide a mixing area for blending colors.

Several programs allow you to mix colors on custom palettes, just as you would with tube paints at an easel. Such features, however, work best on computers equipped with 24-bit full-color graphic display cards where you have the most realistic color capabilities.

The Paint Bucket tool lets you fill an area with color quickly. If you touch the bucket to an area of like pixels, it changes those pixels to whatever color you loaded in the bucket.

The Blend tool is like the Paint Bucket, but it allows you to lay down a gradient fill that is a blend of the foreground and background colors you selected. You can determine the direction of the fill with a couple of clicks of the mouse or stylus. In Photoshop you can add a gradient fill to any shape or letter you wish by clicking on it with the Magic Wand tool.

The Paint Bucket, Brush, Airbrush, and other rendering tools get charged with whatever colors you select from the palette or the image itself using the Eyedropper tool.

SPECIAL PURPOSE AND EFFECTS FILTERS

Special purpose and correction filters correct, enhance or otherwise improve your image or a selected portion of the image. On the other hand, some of these filters can also be used to extract line art from scanned images.

Image-editing programs also have some astonishing special effects that can change an entire image or portions of an image. Some special effects work in gray-scale as well as with color images. In Photoshop, these are called Stylize Filters and are found on the Filter menu.

In Photoshop a few effects are available in the Image menu under the Map commands. These commands are used to modify the entire pixelmap that is your image. Posterize, for example, allows you to convert your image into any number of contrast levels, particularly useful when preparing photos for spot-color and silk-screen imaging. Thresholding reduces a photographic image to black and white.

Faceting, Crystalizing and Mosaic filters create sharp definition by regrouping pixels of similar color or value. The Faceting filter groups pixels into blocks of like-colored pixels, whereas the Crystallize filter organizes them into polygons or

Catherine Schmeltz and Crit Warren, untitled
Schmeltz and Warren took all the photos they used to create this illustration in Photoshop for the cover of the Ohio College Association brochure, "Toward College in Ohio 92/93."

Daniel Rodgers, "Tesla"
A scan of a black-and-white woodcut was colorized and processed in Photoshop to create this image.

Many other filters provide interesting effects. Here's a rundown of some of the standard options that come with most of the popular image-editing programs:
• Diffuse throws your image out of focus.
• Emboss creates an embossed, three-dimensional effect.
• Find Edges and Trace Contour turn your image into a line drawing, tracing the edges and borders in your image, and outlining them.
• Fragment creates four copies of the image and offsets them from each other, very much like a photographic star filter.
• Pointillist or Impressionist filters convert your image into thousands of colored dots.
• Solarize creates a blend between your image's negative and positive areas.

Aldus Gallery Effects, which you can use with image-editing as well as painting programs, also offers a series of special effects to provide even more options for image enhancement and distortion.

SHARPEN, BLUR AND DISTORTION FILTERS

You've got a fuzzy shot, or a portion of your photo is slightly out of focus. The Sharpen command can help. You may discover, however, that too much sharpening can hurt as much as it helps. Because the process of sharpening involves remapping pixels to sharpen the naturally occurring edges in an image, the image also degrades somewhat, appearing pixelated or speckled. You can use a despeckle filter, but it's likely to just blur your image again. Badly out-of-focus images aren't improved much through successive sharpening.

However, the Sharpen feature is handy for adding clarity to slightly out-of-focus portraits. A photographer once told me that the most important feature is a person's eyes,

hexagons, similar to the appearance of a cut gemstone. The mosaic filter allows you to determine the block size in pixels. TV programs often employ this effect when obscuring the identity of someone.

You can also add noise to an image, and I don't mean a sound track. "Noise" is a computer graphics term that means adding a random pattern of pixels over an image to add texture, create a new value, or give your image a painterly look.

so just concentrate on focusing the clarity of your subject's eyes.

Blur filters such as the Gaussian Blur in Photoshop can create an ethereal haze or soften the edges on a photo you feel is too sharp. Motion blurring can also be achieved to simulate a sudden movement such as an athlete in motion. Radial blurring is ideal for vignetting an image or giving part of an image a "celestial glow."

Pinch, Ripple, Spherize, Twirl and Wave filters can distort an image in the way that each name implies with interesting results.

COLOR EFFECTS

You may want to convert your gray-scale images to color images. The variously shaded gray pixels have equivalent, corresponding shades of color that can be adjust-ed with the HSL (Hue, Saturation and Lightness) and HSB (Hue, Saturation and Brightness) modes. Don't expect to apply realistic color to a black-and-white photo, but you can achieve a hand-colored look.

Image-editing programs also allow you to convert images into duotones, tritones and quad-tones— color models that limit the range of color to produce a special effect. This is particularly useful with gray-scale images. The presence of one or two more colors in the rendering of a black-and-white photograph can produce some dramatic and pleasing effects. When you output your duotone image to a raster image processor like a Linotronic imagesetter, the second, third and fourth colors will be offset from one another.

Alan Brown, "John"
Brown used a scan of an SX-70 Polaroid as a base for the creation of a painterly image in Photoshop for this self-promotional piece.

**Sergio Spada,
"Mysterious Passageways"**
Created in Photoshop from scanned
photographs.

FILE FORMATS

Image/photo-editing programs provide for saving your images for importing and exporting in a number of file formats. These include:

TIFF (Tag Image File Format): A high-resolution, digitized image file that contains a display image or "tag" that can be imported into a page-layout or graphics program for positioning in the document. The file also contains the high-resolution output information that is sent to the output device (printer).

RIFF (Raster Image File Format): The PC-based image-editing program counterpart to TIFF.

PICT/PICT2: File formats produced by drawing programs with stored information in Quick-Draw formulas. They can be interpreted by Quick-Draw or PostScript printers. PICT2 images contain language that enables them to be output on color printers or imagesetters.

EPSF (Encapsulated PostScript Format): A file format that allows PostScript files to be stored, edited and transferred between programs and output to any PostScript-driven device. EPSF files contain a display image and a printer code image.

Scitex: This format allows your image to be color separated on a high-end Scitex workstation computer. Although the other major high-end system manufacturers, Crosfield and Hell, can accommodate files from your image-editing software, they must be read as TIFF, RIFF or EPSF files. Again, confer with your client and/or service bureau to determine which format is best.

GIF: CompuServe, the worldwide subscription network that connects Macs, PCs and God knows what else in a vast network of computers, has adopted GIF as a means of allowing users to interchange and display graphic image files. The files are display bit-maps without the high-resolution information necessary for editing.

Amiga ILF/ILBN: Formats readable on the Amiga platform.

MacPaint: This format enables you to further manipulate your image in MacPaint or similar bit-map editing programs. If you prepare an image that will be viewed on a Macintosh-compatible notebook computer with one-bit display, save your image in MacPaint format.

Perhaps this scenario can help illustrate how you will typically work with file formats:

You scan a color photograph and save it as a PICT file, which you can open in Adobe Photoshop for manipulation. You also scan a piece of line art, which you save as a TIFF. Both of these elements will be combined later in the page layout program PageMaker.

Next, you open Photoshop and then open the PICT file, which is displayed on the screen for you to manipulate, retouch or rescale. Since you are working on a composition that will be printed commercially, you convert the file from RGB (red, green, blue) to CMYK. This critical maneuver allows you to see colors on your screen truer to process-color output because your computer automatically adjusts your display for CMYK representation.

After you manipulate your image, you save it for transfer to your page-layout program where it will be integrated with elements of type and the TIFF image you scanned earlier. Before you quit Photoshop you save your file as an EPSF. A dialog box comes up, giving you more precise information (and a few more choices) on how to configure your EPSF file. Your file is now saved as five separate files. Four of those files will be used to create the separation films—

Cyan, Magenta, Yellow and Black. The fifth file is a composite of the image that you will place in your page-layout program.

Now you're in PageMaker with your document open, and you use the Place command to place your composite EPSF image file. Remember, your other four files should not be thrown out, moved or tampered with. They should stay with your PageMaker document wherever it goes, especially to your output service bureau. Your software will call for the visual information that these files contain, and integrate the image files into film separations.

Finally, you place your TIFF image in the same document. This is a simple black-and-white line drawing that requires no further manipulation. It can be imported directly into your page layout using the Place command.

YOUR GATEWAY TO FOUR-COLOR REPRODUCTION

Your image-editing software is a means of preparing your image for final, four-color reproduction. It

Michael Johnson, untitled
This painting, used in a DGWB & Ulead print ad, was created in Aldus Photostyler running on a computer with an Intel 486/50 processor, MS DOS 5.0, 16MB RAM and a 400MB hard disk. The photographic elements that make up the composition were scanned on a Microtek flatbed scanner.

Dana Trousil, "Galactic Mandolin"
Trousil painted and manipulated this image in Photoshop; no scanning was involved. It will be used as a cover illustration on a CD record for musician and composer Radin Zenkl.

will enable you to take a full-color image from another program and prepare it in the appropriate color mode (CMYK) and file format for best reproduction.

For example, if you prepare a full-color image in a program like Fractal Design Painter, it's usually a good idea to examine your final illustration in your image-editing program because it has useful color separation tools, and superior screen-setting algorithms for producing a better image. This may change, of course, if rendering programs are further developed to offer more sophisticated output tools.

In the real world of computer-based publishing, your images will likely be integrated into a page layout program like QuarkXPress, Aldus PageMaker, Frame, Ventura Publisher, Design Studio, etc. Consequently, your image must be prepared in a file format compatible with these programs so you or your

client can access and print it.

If you produce graphics for publication, you probably have some familiarity with high-end pre-press systems such as Scitex, Crosfield and Hell that support high dpi scans and output. These systems have the capability to integrate images and typography at extremely high resolutions—much higher than those attained by desktop systems—for output to film negatives and print reproduction. Most of these high-end publishing systems accept files produced on the Mac and PC with off-the-shelf desktop publishing and illustration software.

I work with service bureaus that offer this technology, and they can deliver the high-quality, high-resolution images and color separations that are required by slick, high-volume publications. However, I have also experimented with my own desktop scanning equipment, Photoshop software and out-

James Dowlen, "Gothic"
Dowlen combines photographic elements with his own renderings to create often startling visual effects.

put from my neighborhood Linotronic service bureau. When I have a client on a shoestring budget who wants color, I usually offer this less expensive path. Often I can deliver a full-color design for the price of a two- or three-color job. And frankly, I'm just as proud of my desktop scans as I am of much of my imagery that was produced on a high-end system.

I don't think I'm going out on a limb here, but in my opinion, desktop technology is improving at such a pace that you may not need to depend on a high-end, expensive system for best quality results. Desktop scanners are becoming more powerful. File sizes are becoming manageable, computers more powerful, and pre-press software better.

Often you must start an image-editing or manipulating project with a less-than-perfect photograph. In this study I have a photograph of a vintage 1960s Mustang that I will make into a T-shirt design. The photo was taken at an outdoor auto show and has a number of distracting or unacceptable elements that must be eliminated before I can use it.

After I've cleaned up the Mustang, I'll combine it in PageMaker with some decorative type that I've already created in Aldus FreeHand. The design will not be silk-screened onto T-shirts. Instead, the final graphic will be output as a paper print that will be turned into a special heat transfer prepared on a Canon Color Copier.

I'll begin the project by scanning in the photograph. My image-editing software, Adobe Photoshop, contains built-in scanner controls that allow me to capture images directly. From within Photoshop on my Mac, I can open my scanner's control panel directly on screen from a pull-down menu. This saves me from having to open a scanning program,

save the image for export, close the scanning program and then reopen the image in an image-editing program. Most popular scanners offer software drivers that work with a variety of image-editing software in much the same manner.

My first objective is to remove the background elements from the photo and clean up the image of the car. Although I won't be manipulating the image, I will use quite a few of the basic tools in an image-editing program. I'll use the Eyedropper to pick up color in one section and apply it to another. I'll retouch several areas with the Rubber Stamp tool as well as work with the Airbrush, Brush and Eraser tools. Both the Marquee tool and the Pen, a precision selecting tool, will be used. As you'll see in this demonstration, there are often several ways you can approach a task. You'll save yourself time and hassles if you always stop to think through a process *before* you start work, so you can choose the best way to go about it.

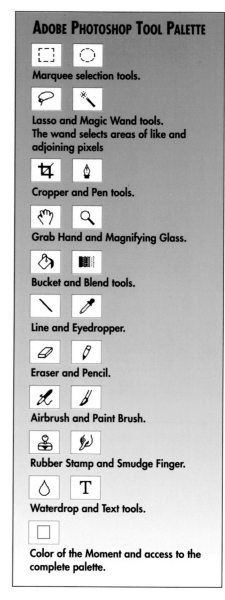

ADOBE PHOTOSHOP TOOL PALETTE

Marquee selection tools.

Lasso and Magic Wand tools. The wand selects areas of like and adjoining pixels

Cropper and Pen tools.

Grab Hand and Magnifying Glass.

Bucket and Blend tools.

Line and Eyedropper.

Eraser and Pencil.

Airbrush and Paint Brush.

Rubber Stamp and Smudge Finger.

Waterdrop and Text tools.

Color of the Moment and access to the complete palette.

1. The original scan of the Ford Mustang was captured in Adobe Photoshop with a flatbed color scanner and a Macintosh. The shot was taken at an outdoor auto show. Our task is to retouch the image of the car, eliminating the distracting elements (like the Garfield in the back window and the dice on the rear-view mirror). Then we will completely eliminate the background and the parking lot surface on which the car rests. But first, we must fix the brightness and contrast of the photo and adjust the overall color balance.

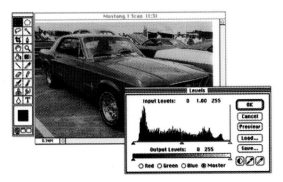

2. To adjust the overall brightness and contrast of the photo, access the Levels histogram under the Image menu. Move sliders until you get the look you want.

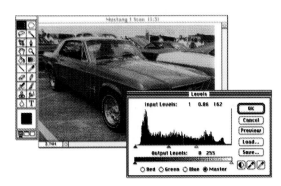

3. Note how the input levels changed numerically as I moved the two sliders to the left a little. Only concentrate on improving the contrast of the element you wish to save, like the car. Don't worry what happens to the rest of the photo.

4. Access the color balance controls and, by moving the sliders, we can make the red warmer by favoring the magenta and yellow while reducing the cyan and green.

5. The car's edge might disappear when we eliminate the background. Using the eyedropper, we sample some color from the hood, load the airbrush, and spray in some light color to define the car's edges.

6. There is a light pole reflected in the hood of the car. This is a job for the rubber stamp tool. Just stamp an area you want repeated...

7. ...and the light pole disappears! The rubber stamp tool is the most powerful and productive tool in your image-editing software. It frequently saves you from having to meticulously airbrush or color match an area you want retouched.

8. The tag and dice on the rear-view mirror must go. The stamp tool won't work effectively in those hard-to-reach areas. It looks like we'll have to do some good old-fashioned rendering with the brush and airbrush.

9. The rubber stamp tool is doing a good job of eliminating that Garfield on the back window. Selecting an obscure pattern to repeat over the cat is a start, but as we continue to assess the entire back window situation we will overspray with an airbrush. Access to tight spots is facilitated by using the magnification tool and working with a brush tool.

10. True, we are using a computer to perform artistic endeavors such as brush rendering and airbrush work. However, an artist with any skills or experience with traditional tools will have an *advantage* working with the computer. Knowing what "looks correct" will contribute to an overall better image.

11. Now we can start eliminating the background. Use the marquee tool and eraser for large areas. For more precision and better results, use the brush tool charged with white paint. It's a tedious job, but there's a better way to cut the Mustang from the background.

12. With the pen selection tool, you can lay precise vector points along a path, adjust the points to fit the curves and corners, then make your cut. Paste the object in a new window with a different background or, in the case below, plain white.

13. Once the image has been saved in a compatible file format, you can combine the graphic with other graphic elements in a program like PageMaker or Quark. The letters were prepared in Aldus FreeHand.

PERMISSIONS

I N D E X

Aldus FreeHand, printing from, 114-115
  See also Drawing programs
Amiga ILF/ILBN, 50, 141
Analog signals, 18
Animation, features for, 18

Backup drive, 16
Bézier curves, 43, 45-46, 133
Billboards, design of, 64
Bit-map, 29, 30, 43, 127-128
  image, demonstrations using, 74-77, 122-125
  in painting programs, 81

CD-ROM, 16
Choke, 114-115
Color
  calibration, 113-114
  comps, 23
  graphics boards, 19-20
  image formatting, 50
  images, registration of, 114-115
  in drawing programs, 62-63
  in image-editing, 135-139
  separations, 114
  spot, in Aldus FreeHand, 51
  spot, in printing, 114
  See also Printer; Display monitor; Microcomputer; Graphics card
Color output
  alternatives to, 26
  an economic approach to, 142-143
  from service bureau, 26
  to slides, 26
Color specification, for service bureau output, 112-113
Commodore Amiga, 6, 34-35, 111
Compact disks. *See* CD-ROM
CompuServe, 140-141
Co-processor board, 17
CPU
  defined, 16
  speed of, 117

Digital signals, 18
Digitization, of an image, 127-128
Disk
  floppy, 16
  hard, 16-17
  read-and-write optical, 16
  removable hard, 16
Display monitor
  calibration, 113-114
  color in, 18
  image bowing, 21
  registration, 21

resolution of, 62
screen flicker, 20-21
shopping for, 18, 20-22
types of, 18
Drafting. *See* Software, drafting; Drafting programs
Drafting programs
  advantages and disadvantages of, 47-48
  how they work, 43
Drawing
  on pressure-sensitive tablet, 27-28, 63, 91, 133
  tools, 68-71
  with pen, 27-28, 63
  See also Software, drawing; Painting
Drawing devices, types of, 16
Drawing/painting programs
  how they work, 43-44
  demonstration of, 54-59
Drawing paths, defined, 71
Drawing programs
  advantages and disadvantages of, 47-48
  Aldus FreeHand demonstration, 74-77
  and color specification, 62-63
  how they work, 43, 61-79
  MacDraw demonstration, 40-41
  PostScript, 43, 74-77, 78-79
  See also Aldus FreeHand

Encapsulated PostScript Files. *See* EPS file
EPS file, 50, 90, 140-141
EPSF. *See* EPS file

Fashion, design of, 68
  See also Software, ModaCAD
Fax modem. *See* Output devices
File compression, 117-120
File formats, types defined, 50-51, 90, 140-141
  See also Image-editing programs
File formatting, 48
Film recorder, 109-110
Frame buffer, defined, 16
Frame rate. *See* Vertical scan rate

GIF (Graphic Image Files), 140-141
Graphics card
  color in, 19
  defined, 16
  gray scale, 19
  number of bits, 19
  purchasing, 18
Graphics display board. *See* Graphics

card; Color
Graphics program, Aldus FreeHand demonstration, 54-59
  See also Aldus FreeHand
Gray scale, on display boards, 19

High-resolution
  drawing programs, 61
  printing devices, 61
  printing, defined, 61

Icons. *See* Onscreen tools
Image-editing programs
  Adobe Photoshop demonstration, 144-147
  file formats for, 140-141
  filters for special effects, 137-139
  techniques for, 130, 132-136
  to improve photographic quality, 138-139
  tools for, 132-136
  See also Software
Import/export, how to, 90

Laser printers, non-PostScript, 22
  See also PostScript, laser printers
Layering
  in drawing software, 66-68
  in software, 45
Logo design, 36-39

MacPaint file format, 51, 141
Mass storage unit, 16
Megabytes, 13, 16
Memory, how much to buy, 16-17
Memory units. *See* Disk
Microcomputer
  color considerations, 13
  customization of, 15
  determining your needs, 14-15
  evaluation of, 13-14
  main components of, 16
  speed of, 17-18
Modem, 16, 100
  and file compression, 117
  See also Output devices
Moiré pattern, fixing of, 116-117
Motherboard, 17
Mouse
  alternatives to, 63
  optical, for drawing, 27
  selection of, 27
Multimedia, features for, 18
Multiscan. *See* Multisynchronous monitor
Multisynchronous monitor, 18

Networking
    and choosing software, 52
    as a backup device, 16
Newsletter banner design, 40-41

Object-oriented graphics. *See* Software, drafting
Onscreen tools
    auto-trace, 54, 56-57, 69-71, 74-75, 122-125
    color blend, 43, 78-79, 92-97
    color fill, 48
    fill demonstrations, 58-59, 76-77
    fills, 43, 68, 92-97, 104-106
    fills in image-editing, 136
    See also Drawing, tools; Painting, tools
Output
    Linotronic, 116
    of color iamges, 26
    problems at the service bureau, 111-117
    to service bureaus, 22, 26
    to slides, 26
    See also Color; Service bureau; Printer; Video
Output devices
    fax modem, 22, 110
    shopping for, 22
    See also Printer; Color; PostScript
Overprinting. *See* Trap

Paint programs, high-resolution, 44-45
    See also Software, painting; Painting programs
Painting
    special effects, 83-85
    tools, 81-84
    See also Software, painting
Painting programs
    advantages and disadvantages of, 46-47
    color special effects, 86-90
    DeskPaint demonstration, 54-59, 122-125
    FullPaint demonstration, 36-39
    how they work, 43, 81-107
    how to begin, 85-86
    PixelPaint demonstration, 92-97, 122-125
    quality of type in, 43
    SuperPaint, 43-44
    working with color in, 86
Photo retouching, 7
Photographic manipulation, software for, 127
Photography, manipulation and editing of, 127-147
    See also Image-editing; Software; Pixels; Scanning; Digitization
PICT/PICT2, 50, 90, 140-141
Pixelmap. *See* Bit-map
Pixels, 127-128

as an illustrative element, 53
    manipulating, 134-139
PostScript, 51
    color problem in drawing programs, 113
    fonts, 33
    for high-resolution, 22
    for output, 22
    laser printers, 22
    See also Drawing programs; PostScript
Pre-press technology, compatibility with, 110
Pressure-sensitive tablet. *See* Drawing
Printer, 16
    color, 22-23
    color comps from, 23
    color laser, 25, 109
    color phase change, 24
    continuous tone die sublimation, 24
    high-resolution ink-jet, 25
    laser, 22, 109
    wax, 23-24
    See also Software
Programs
    Fractal Design Painter, 91
    Microsoft Windows, 13
    ModaCAD, 25

RAM, 13, 16-17
Random Access Memory. *See* RAM
Raster Image File Format. *See* RIFF
Raster Image Processor. *See* RIP
Resolution, for proper scanning, 128-132
RIFF, 50, 90, 140
RIP, 61
ROM. *See* CD-ROM

Scanner, 6, 16, 29-32
    color, 31-32
    costs of, 31-32
    gray-scale, 31
    how one works, 29-30
    resolution of, 31-32
    selection of, 30-31
    service bureau use of, 109
    software for, 30
Scanning
    and copyright infringement, 6
    demonstration of, 122-125
    determining dpi for, 32, 128-132
    for image editing, 33
    to manipulate photographs, 127-132
Scitex, and other high-end formats, 140
Screen. *See* Display monitor
Service bureau, 109-121
    and color calibration, 113-114
    and illegal software problems, 110-111
    and incompatible font files, 111
    and incompatible software, 111

and viruses, 111
    charges at, 120-121
    color output specification, 112-113
    common problems with, 111-117
    hardware used by, 109-110
    software used by, 110-111
Software
    choosing, 51-53
    differences between programs, 45-48, 61-63, 81
    drafting, 32
    drafting/painting, 32-33
    drawing, 32, 40-41, 61-79, 74-77
    drawing, painting, and image editing, 7-9
    for file compression, 119
    image-editing, 33, 113-114, 127-147
    memory requirements of, 16-17
    painting, 32, 36-39, 43-44, 54-59, 81-107
    programs, speed of, 17
    service bureau compatibility, 111
    types of programs to buy, 32-34
    See also Drawing; Drawing programs; Painting; Drawing/Painting; Image-editing
Stylus. *See* Drawing, with pen

Tag Image File Format. *See* TIFF
Techniques, creating texture, 98-107
    See also Drawing; Drawing programs; Painting; Painting programs; Onscreen tools; Layering
TIFF, 50, 90, 140-141
Tiling, 104, 53
Tools. *See* Onscreen tools
Trap, 114-115
Turnkey systems, 117
Type font, 33-34
    disadvantages in painting programs, 47
    incompatibility at service bureau, 111

Vector graphics. *See* Software, drafting; Drafting programs
Vertical scan rate, 20-21
Video
    importation, 18
    output, 26
    still, 6-7